LIFE AND SOLITUDE IN EASTER ISLAND

by

DR. DARÍO VERDUGO-BINIMELIS

Bloomington, IN Milton Keynes, UK

authorHOUSE®

AuthorHouse™
1663 Liberty Drive, Suite 200
Bloomington, IN 47403
www.authorhouse.com
Phone: 1-800-839-8640

AuthorHouse™ UK Ltd.
500 Avebury Boulevard
Central Milton Keynes, MK9 2BE
www.authorhouse.co.uk
Phone: 08001974150

First published by AuthorHouse 2/13/2007

ISBN: 978-1-4259-8228-7 (sc)
ISBN: 978-1-4259-8227-0 (hc)

Printed in the United States of America
Bloomington, Indiana

This book is printed on acid-free paper.

Library of Congress Control Number: 2006910635

*To my beloved wife Adriana, and to my sons Pedro, Dario,
Roberto and Gonzalo, for all their support and sustenance in
this grand family adventure to Easter Island.*

*In remembrance to my parents, Peyo and Carmelita and
Adriana's parents Alberto and Adriana who suffered with our
remote absence.*

*To my old "Pascuense friends"… the time and distance have not
erased them from my heart.*

Contents

FOREWORD

It is not easy to preface this book written by my dear friend, Dr. Darío Verdugo-Binimelis, as it does not represent a traditional narrative. I view this as a very special literary work that reflects his experiences expressed from the bottom of his heart during the two years he spent with his family in this enigmatic island in the vast South Pacific—the "most "island" of the islands of the world". The place, also known to its natives as Rapa Nui, is, after all, the most isolated place on Earth[1]. When we place such isolation within the 1950s time frame, in which there was absolutely no airline service, only a few sailings a year and virtually no radio communication, we begin to better understand the implications of the decision made by Dr. Verdugo when he applied for medical duty to such an unimaginably remote speck. Of course, those of us who knew Darío were not surprised when we learned of his strong determination to travel with his family to the "world's navel", as this mysterious volcanic island is also referred.

In a sense, this book, *Life and Solitude in Easter Island*, was actually written by the author from the bottom of his heart the day he departed from his beloved island. But he did not attempt to write it then because, I feel, he wanted to share his memories with his dear family first. He then waited almost fifty years to decide to gather all his notes and organize his thoughts in a narrative "prior to having those memories fade away," as he tells us. I believe, however, that the principal reason for letting us all learn about such extraordinary adventure comes from his profound generosity—a generosity to share with all of us the spectacular challenges that he faced in Easter Island as a medical doctor, teacher, advisor and caring family man.

---

[1] It is the easternmost island of Polynesia, the vast archipelago between Australia and South America. Its closest neighbors are the Gambier Islands in French Polynesia, at a distance of more than 1550 miles (2500 km). The Chilean coast is more than 1860 miles (3000 km) away.

There is no doubt that Dr. Verdugo, in addition to being a good physician, is an excellent narrator. A journey starting from his "Beginnings of an Adventure", to the sailings "Between Sky and Sea", and to the arrival on the island, are all truly documentaries. The reflections contained in this book, narrated by the observing eye of a towering *moai,* takes the reader through a time capsule that brings to life the landing of king Hotu Matua with his entourage on the eastern beaches that in those days were surrounded by "gigantic palm" trees everywhere. These mariners and their descendants became tireless in creating and erecting enormous stone figures known as *moais.* Thus the history unfolds, viewed through the philosophical eye of the moai, who unflinchingly observes the arrival of the second wave of navigators. The moai also witnesses a period of history from the wars among two prevailing cultures and tribal disputes, all the way through the western discovery of the island by the arrival of a Dutch navigator. This European discovery constitutes an historical milestone for that community from that day on; this remote land came to be known as Easter Island. The moai also witnesses the successive arrivals of other large vessels with strange people on board. Sometimes the visitors had good intentions and on other occasions bad ones, but they all helped shape the uncertain destiny faced by the island's inhabitants. The author highlights, through his moai, the arrival of Christianity in 1864 through Father Eugenio Eyraud, a member of the Sacred Heart Congregation. Twenty-two years later, in 1886, the island became a possession of Chile.

The most noteworthy aspects of Dr. Verdugo's book, however, come from the narrative of his daily routine. Those narratives range from the formal family sessions held at his home, to the contemplation of spectacular sunsets, to the joint efforts with his wife, Adriana, to establish home schooling for their children. Everything is livened up with anecdotes related to the daily contacts with the Pascuenses of that period, who were full of joy and naïve ingenuity. The Pascuenses of that time had never been exposed to the use of currency, alcohol, nor tobacco. The author also tells us about the climate, geography, flora and fauna of the island, as well as the psychology of the natives: the Pascuense.

The author's experience as a medical doctor is not only interesting, but it is of great historical and scientific value. Dr. Verdugo had to perform his practice in an environment in which most everything was lacking, making it difficult to deliver adequate medical services—from dealing with birth complications to bone fractures, etc. His description of a virulent measles epidemic which erupted in 1953 is very vivid; this event caused him many sleepless nights. The most impressive medical aspect, however, is to read about Dr. Verdugo's dealings with a disease that has been feared since biblical times: leprosy. The leprosy on Easter Island existed within a society suffering from poverty, reminiscent of Father Damian de Veuster, the sainted martyr of Molokai, who during the last century dedicated himself to the leper colonies of Hawaii and died from the disease himself. Perhaps not as dramatically, Dr. Verdugo had to overcome the fear of contamination, and, encouraged by his vocation and his enduring faith in God, he was truly able to help and care for the handful of patients in the leper colony of Rapa Nui.

The author had the opportunity to meet several personalities who besides Father Eyraud (1828-1868) have marked milestones in the history of Rapa Nui. The first one was the legendary Father Sebastian Englert (1885-1969); the Chaplain of the island who shared his monumental work titled, "The land of *Hotu Matua*," and lived on the island from 1935 until his death. Dr. Verdugo also refers to the teacher, Lorenzo Baeza-Vega, who later passed away during one of the visits of the explorer Thor Heyerdahal, when one of the boats full of students that were being taken to visit Heyerdahal's vessel capsized in the Anakena Bay. Professor Baeza drowned while trying to save his students. Due to this heroic act, the school on the island bears his name today. The other personality that Dr. Verdugo mentions is Alberto Hotus, the navy nurse at that time. This Pascuense became a great defender of the cultural heritage of the island. He became mayor and today is one of the most influential members of the Advisory Board for the senior citizens on the island.

In writing this book, Dr. Verdugo makes an urgent call to the Chilean authorities to adapt policies aimed at preserving, not only the cultural heritage, but also the Rapa Nui society, which each day is becoming more overrun from the overwhelming increase in immigration from the mainland. The natives now represent a minority of the island's population.

The reader who decides to travel to Rapa Nui today will not find the island as it was painted by the author with his master literary strokes. He will have, however, a very valuable reference of what such a marvelous island was like half a century ago.

Dear Dr. Verdugo, Adriana and descendants:

What you all did, what you saw and what you have memorialized in this book has not been in vain. The community of Rapa Nui, as well as Chileans and foreigners, who love this island, will remember your writings forever with great gratitude. They represent the guarantors of the island's heritage—Easter Island is now a National Monument in addition to its status of humanity's patrimony, and UNESCO has declared it a "Biosphere Reserve". Without a doubt, the values that are uncovered here will therefore be carefully guarded for the well-being of humanity.

This book is a generous gift which the author has shared with all of us, and I can assure the readers that they will truly enjoy it and experience moments of exquisite emotion while reading it.

Dr. Juan Grau V.
Secretary General of the Ecological Institute of Chile
Santiago, January of 1998

From the translators...

I am Dario Jr., one of the protagonists of this story living in the United States for more than half of my life. I very much wanted to share my father's book with my family and friends, so it was natural to translate it into English.

When we began this project a couple years ago we divided the task among the five of us: Barbara provided valuable overall review, while our daughters Lindsay, Julie and Diana tackled specific chapters.

Jennifer Palonus-Simonds, Barbara's sister, contributed enormously to the final manuscript by improving its style; her experiences as editor and her creative mind became priceless.

While translating this book by us non-professional writers grew into a daunting undertaking, it was a valuable learning experience for all of us, and brought back to me fond memories from my childhood, and a true appreciation for our parents' generosity in providing an experience we could never duplicate.

WHY I WROTE THIS BOOK

I originally thought that the experiences that filled our lives and constituted our grand adventure in such a remote island for two years would be only shared with our family and closest friends. Nearly half a century later, however, I decided to write this book out of fear of forgetting these memories, as they tend to get left behind and I could see them gradually fading away with the passage of time. I wanted to memorialize the wonderful years of our "Rapa Nui existence," with tropical as well as mild winter days, with happiness as well as sadness, with hope as well as despair, but always with the solid base of our family. In such isolation and remoteness, our close family ties strengthened further, bringing us much happiness and making into reality those words from that old song: "home, sweet home, there is no other place like home".

Living on a remote Polynesian island in the South Pacific, with no communication with the external world and within a totally different cultural paradigm, we had to communicate among ourselves more intimately. Within that loneliness, we were not only brought closer together as a family, but in this humble and limited environment we had the opportunity to enrich our spiritual and cultural lives.

I do not want those memories to fade away, and through these pages I want my sons, now grown men with their own families, to relive that period of their formative years which have had so much influence on the formation of their characters. They can then tell their offspring that when they were children, they dreamed about a life full of adventures, with pirates and vessels in remote islands – emulating Robinson Crusoe – and many times those juvenile fantasies became reality in their lives in Easter Island.

An additional factor that motivated me to undertake these writings is my nostalgic feelings for the island. I felt that by transcribing my melancholic feelings from past memories into this book, it has been a true therapy, allowing me to relive that nostalgia.

From another perspective, I would like to be able to awaken the conscience of our leadership in Chile. I feel there is need to consider substantial revision of public policy, in order to avoid the gradual destruction of the culture and language of the Pascuenses.

Finally, I have written this book to reflect on the lessons learned from the history of Rapa Nui, which have not been sufficiently appreciated. The history tells us of the destruction of its natural resources from over-consumption, many centuries ago, with all its severe consequences. It is virtually impossible not to compare what happened in this speck of land, lost in the immensity of the Pacific Ocean, with what could occur on our Planet Earth. This planet, which is a small island within the vast universe, could be ravaged if we continue to exploit it in the way we do today due to negligence and insufficient environmental knowledge by the human race.

And so I have written this book, with notes from those days, including medical files I had, material I have studied, and long conversations with my wife, Adriana, recollecting and rebuilding our "Pascuense life". This book is not intended to be a scientific nor an historical text, nor have I intended to make it a literary piece, since I would be incapable of doing so. I only relate the experiences of a family – **my family** – transplanted onto a faraway island - the most remote and isolated island in this world. I also share, in the most objective way possible, what I saw, heard and what I learned on Rapa Nui. Finally, toward the end of the book I express my concerns about the way in which the affairs of Easter Island are being conducted today.

If I am able to have my children remember part of their upbringing while reading these lines, if I am able to have my friends join me retrospectively in this adventure of my life, if I am able to mitigate somewhat my nostalgia, and finally, if I am able to foster debate and bring awareness as to the potential threat of our natural resources in the world and the Pascuense culture, I will be satisfied. I could not ask for anything else as I write this narrative.

Dr. Darío Verdugo-Binimelis
"Taote"[2]

---

[2] Title for the Doctor in the Polynesian language used in Easter Island – a position of high honor within the island community.
Dr. Verdugo was the sole *Taote* on the island.

Chapter One

The Beginning of an Adventure

Nothing could be more ironic than to have to credit the staid, conservative *El Mercurio* newspaper for inspiring me, my wife, and four sons to live on a remote Polynesian island. I would never have believed this; and I must express my appreciation to that venerable journal for setting in motion an unforgettable adventure.

It was a Sunday in early November, 1952 (late spring in Santiago, Chile) when my wife, Adriana, who was browsing through *El Mercurio* for some movies to see that afternoon, ran into an announcement from the Ministry of Health soliciting applications for the position of the sole physician resident for Easter Island. The announcement, dated November 7, 1952, indicated that the ship was scheduled to sail December 2, a mere 25 days away. I was sitting in my favorite couch settled into the characteristic afternoon lull. Perhaps she was thinking that such opportunity could be more exciting than any movie being shown in town that weekend, or maybe it was her restless temperament in tune with mine, or her adventurous spirit driven by her Portuguese ancestry of explorers, that made her say with the same tone as suggesting a movie: "Why don't we all go to Easter Island?"

There has never been a Sunday afternoon program that was going to transform our lives into a two-year life experience that could have been better received by my family. Perhaps a possible sojourn to Polynesia was more exciting than the last movie premier—and would we be the actors ourselves? I responded "yes" before I even had a chance to be fully awakened from that afternoon lull. And from that moment on began the most fantastic adventure that we could ever imagine. It became reality accompanied by our sons Pedro, Darío, Roberto and Gonzalo, whose ages ranged between nine and twelve years old.

What a tempting offer it seemed to apply for such a great opportunity in Easter Island for both my family and my medical profession! On this warm Sunday afternoon in Santiago, we could really dream of the fresh, deep blue water of the South Pacific. In our imaginations we could see thick tropical trees protecting us from the Sun. Furthermore, we would ask ourselves: 'Why do we have to live and stay permanently in the same place when the world is so large and beautiful?' At times we felt romantically identified as citizens of the world, of an ideal world without borders—cozy, which opens its meridians and parallels, like immense arms—beckoning us to travel. How could we resist those temptations to explore new horizons?

Considering that only moments ago I was half asleep dreaming, and now awaken letting the reigns of my imagination go unconstrained! How wonderful to imagine getting away from the daily routine, leaving behind the stress of modern life! How fantastic it is to abandon the imprisonment of civilization, leaving the congestion of Santiago's inadequate public transportation[3], the queues for the rationing of basic goods that existed in the early '50s: ranging from milk, butter, and sugar, to kerosene and other necessities, and the rude behavior of people when faced with scarcity! Wouldn't it be paradise to live far away from all this urban stress after all?

The next step was for us to start thinking about all the pros and cons of this possible journey. Among the 'pros' were the quick

---

[3] Most professional families, including ours, could not afford to own automobiles

departure from this stressful life in Santiago, with the possibility of fostering a much closer family life, and a unique experience that would serve us well long after our return home to the mainland. Among the 'cons' would be the long-term separation from our parents and friends. And would we miss basic public utilities such as electricity and running water? Would we miss newspapers and magazines, the cultural life of the big urban city? Wouldn't we feel lonely and isolated so far away, where communication with the mainland was only by vessel that traveled once a year on a ten-day crossing?

Adriana and I called our four sons to the weekly family meeting to discuss with them the advantages and disadvantages of this 'project.' The children then immediately began to dream about 'the grand adventure'. The boys would be the real protagonists of this marvelous quest. Yes, they would be not only spectators but the true actors in this adventure—a mix of Robinson Crusoe and Treasure Island! The balance of the scale was swinging from one side to the other, but it eventually tipped toward the 'pros'. The first step of our journey had already been taken. We were convinced that we must accept the call to this adventure, and to leap toward it, being compelled by latent genes from our nomadic ancestors from our human origins. We dismissed the 'cons' of this adventure with exquisite rationalizations and mostly they became irrelevant.

Having made this important joint decision with our family, we told the children that they could not tell anyone about this possible journey as it was not yet certain, and that they should not talk about it in school. If the trip did not materialize, it would simply result in teasing and making fun of them in school. However, enthusiasm overcame the rules, and the next day Roberto was telling his teachers and classmates at school that we were leaving for Easter Island. We learned about this when the school's Father Superior asked our oldest son Pedro to confirm this rumor.

We asked Roberto for an explanation for not following our rules and he apologized with a confusing, but clever, explanation: "Since all teachers would have read the newspaper and noticed the announcement

3

for the doctor's position on Easter Island, they would have concluded that Dad, being a medical doctor, had applied for it." Furthermore, as Roberto has been taught not to lie, he added that when one of the teachers asked him, "Did your father apply for this position?" he could not reply anything but "Yes!" My wife and I couldn't contain our laughter at his creative rationalization, but we made a point of insisting that when we established rules for the children they were to be followed.

Now we faced the second step, which was more complicated. Even though I was nearing the age of 40, we felt that we had to seek our parents' consent for such a drastic family move. We had to convince them on the merits of our decision to move to Easter Island. This would be a wonderful opportunity in spite of the inevitable drawbacks; it would certainly require plenty of persuasion. In deliberations with our respective fathers—more mind than heart—they ended up supporting us, despite the sadness and distance of this assignment, given the valuable opportunities for medicine, human experiences and development. Our mothers, on the other hand—more heart than mind—were skeptical, thinking about the distance, solitude and sadness from the separation. We had to assure our parents that the journey was not dangerous, that the children would not fall behind in their studies and become uncivilized savages. I assured them that as a medical doctor I would maintain high standards and that Adriana would not acquire Polynesian customs, nor would she become socially unfit. We had open deliberations with our parents, to whom we were very close. In these discussions we addressed them formally[4] which was the typical manner of that era. Adriana and I made use of every possible verbal skill to explain the virtues of departing temporarily from our urban civilization. We reassured our parents that there would be no threat of leprosy from the small leper colony on Easter Island, since it is very difficult to acquire the disease without direct physical contact. We lovingly explained we would get to know ourselves better as a family, and it would be so healthy for the children

---

[4] Using the formal 'usted' (you) instead of the familiar 'tu', and 'Don Pedro' and 'Don Alberto'

to live in close contact with nature. At the end of our discussions with our parents, we were able to persuade them for their support, which was not granted without an emotional pain that we deeply shared.

The third step needed to make this trip possible was to be selected among all the other doctor candidates who were applying for this position. There were only three days left to submit the application with my curriculum vitae. I had to gather all the necessary documentation, my diplomas, course certificates, publications, etc., then await the resolution from the nominating committee. It had been many years since I was a student in medical school experiencing that anxious sensation awaiting exam results. That was exactly the way I felt: I was once again at the mercy of the three "examiners" in medical school—who in the old days would place marbles to provide the results of an exam: would they be red (high grades), white (average) or black (fail)? On Thursday at noon I received a phone call in a laconic tone from a civil servant: "You have been selected for the position of physician resident on Easter Island". Only a few days had elapsed since reading the announcement in *el Mercurio* that Sunday afternoon!

That telephone call from the Ministry of Health was effectively the "***BIG*** call"[5]. The impact of the call made the reality of our journey set in! At that moment the dream was instantly replaced by cold, hard facts. The rationalizations faded away—and I became truly scared. I felt lonely and isolated with my loved ones in that mysterious and remote Rapa Nui (the native word for Easter Island), of which so much has been said and written, but which we only knew as a diminutive geographical point situated in the middle of the Pacific Ocean. I was faced with the realities of being transplanted and leaving behind everything that had been associated with our lives, to abandon those things that were part of us: habits, customs, and comforts. I cannot say enough about the sadness that we were feeling to be separated from our dear parents and the sadness that we knew this long separation would cause them. If something were to happen to them during our absence, how would we

---

[5] In Spanish this is called a "telefonaso".

return immediately when there was a ten-day vessel crossing only once a year and we would be separated by a distance of more than 2,600 miles? Wouldn't it be risky to go with the children? And the leprosy, wouldn't there be a danger of contamination? And who would care for me if I needed specialized medical attention? We were full of questions, doubts, and anxiety, but we felt committed and could not stop and unwind everything after what we had done and said so far.

We were facing the greatest adventure of our lives, so we resolved to close our minds to the tragic questions and prepare ourselves in the best possible way to tackle this challenge. We had to find out what to bring and what to leave behind—for which we had advice from numerous "experts" on Easter Island, who always gave us conflicting information![6] We had to acquire books to shorten our long Polynesian days; we had to request from the Chilean Ministry of Education the study syllabus for our children, we needed to move out of our home, store our household items, and return the telephone to the phone company[7], request permission for a leave of absence from my various medical posts at the hospital and the National Railway Company; buy adequate clothing and supplies for island living and a thousand more things to do as we approached the date of departure.

In the meantime, the children were not facing the new realities of this challenge—they were living in a dream. They spoke about an island of savages and pirates, of long vacations and beautiful places without school or exams. They would tell their friends of all the adventures they were about to experience, the long journey by sea…their friends began to look at them with an envious admiration.

The days were advancing rapidly toward our departure and we were able to gradually overcome the fear of the unknown. But then, all of a sudden we were faced with the anguish of reality in which we had to say goodbye, especially to our parents. We could see that day

---

[6] Other than some historical and geographical facts, there was very limited practical information on Easter Island in those days. We knew of no one, nor anybody who knew someone, who had ever visited such a remote speck of land.

[7] Upon returning home to Chile it could take years to re-establish a phone line.

drawing inexorably closer and we almost wished we could jump without transition to transfer instantly from Santiago to Rapa Nui. Time cannot be stopped however, and two days prior to the trip, "the grand journey", we were gathered around an elegant table at the classic Savoy Hotel in downtown Santiago for a farewell supper with our parents, closest relatives and friends, which with all their love they had organized. Everything was elegant and exquisite. The floral arrangements were beautiful and aromatic; the music was evocatively reminiscent of the past; the food was delicious, but we were all sad, very sad, even though we pretended to be happy. We wanted to fool ourselves by laughing, singing and speaking loudly, but there were too many eyes that were fixed wide open to avoid the outburst of tears. I am sure that while we were singing, if for only one moment I had stopped I would have burst into tears. Never in my life have I attended an event so sad, but with such an appearance of joy.

Two days later, we woke up to a cold and cloudy morning, in tune with our spirits. That morning we left Santiago on the 8:00 A.M. express train to the port city of Valparaíso. This was a farewell that was painfully extended in silence during the three-hour train ride to the port city.

Departure of the Verdugo Family to Easter Island
in December, 1952 on the *Allipén*

CHAPTER TWO

BETWEEN SKY AND SEA

Our farewell from Valparaíso was joyful, as we boarded the old steamship the *Allipén*. Our friends from Viña del Mar[8], who we knew from our many happy years living in the 'garden city', where I had been a doctor at Viña's main hospital, surprised us with their joy and good wishes. They were so generous with displays of friendship, gifts and hugs. With all of the commotion, I almost did not notice when the ship began its separation from the pier and slowly departed, proceeding to make its way into the open ocean. Little by little the goodbyes began to disappear and the coast faded away gradually. Valparaíso and Viña del Mar were now far from our sight but not from our hearts. We realized at that moment our true journey had begun.

Life aboard the ship was something completely new to my family. It was reminiscent for me, however, of my days as a medical doctor in the Chilean Navy where I began my career. My wife, Adriana, with her Portuguese roots appeared to adapt very quickly aboard the ship. the *Allipén* was a vessel for passengers and cargo. The officers of

---

[8] Including my medical colleagues and numerous friends from the Rotary Club, where I had been the president.

the ship considered it old but very seaworthy. Its seaworthiness did not, however, compensate for its frugal accommodations.

The cabins were so small that our bags and suitcases practically occupied all of the space between the two berths. Our children were accommodated at the small infirmary, which had four berths and was awfully warm due to its proximity to the ship's blistering chimney and engine room. The endless turning of the steam engine produced a monotonous sound that was difficult to ignore. Adriana and I were a bit uneasy that the boys were on another deck and unsupervised, far from us. To occupy our time during the long days at sea, we would walk and sit at the main deck and socialize in a small room that also served as the officer's mess hall. On the deck it was generally windy and warm, but rather than breathing a typical marine breeze, it was overpowered by the strong odor of garlic coming from the galley. During the first few days it was not easy to get accustomed to the vessel's elegant wallowing in the seaway. Occasionally the ship would shudder with a motion which could be described as swinging its hips. This made us assume that this vessel with so many annual trips to Easter Island had learned Polynesian dances.

The passengers aboard were of varied backgrounds and were very personable. Mr. Daly, a very kind and cordial Brit, was the General Manager of the Easter Island Company[9]. The Company's core business was wool, as the island had a large sheep herd and produced merino wool of the highest quality which was exported to the UK. In this annual voyage, the *Allipén* had to bring the necessary supplies, materials, staples, parcels and other goods for the island natives (Pascuenses). There was also a German priest on board, a former officer in WWI, who spoke enthusiastically of his military adventures. His clergy attire could not even begin to disguise his soldier profile and his military Prussian demeanor. When saying Holy Mass, however, he would mellow and

---

[9] This Company, called "Compañía Explotadora de la Isla de Pascua" (or Company to Exploit Resources of Easter Island), had tremendous influence and power in the island. It could be compared to the arrangement with East India Company in the 18th century.

his spirituality would overtake him, and he became transformed into an apostle of Christ.

Other passengers included a sophisticated French-Canadian diplomat; Marcus Chamudes, a writer and photographer, who had a spirit of curiosity and a great knack for ironic commentary; and an itinerant American, who had lived for an extended period of time in diverse Polynesian islands. The American began introducing us to his stories and adventures in that mysterious world of Polynesia that would become our home for the next two years. This is a remarkable world that, while it is scattered into thousands of tiny islands over a wide extension of the Pacific Ocean, it maintains a cohesive racial and cultural community with similar languages. Also on board there were two officers from the Chilean Navy and the newly appointed Governor of the Island, Captain Carlos Salazar Contreras. He was traveling with his wife, Mirtho, and their four young children, all of whom were very amicable.

Later during the voyage, while we were on the high seas, we became aware that there were two Pascuenses on board who were being returned after having left as stowaways the prior year[10]. The two islanders were being accommodated at the bottom of the ship with the some of the working crew.

Being an old vessel, the *Allipén* did not have a freezer. But that was no reason not to have fresh meat onboard. When we left Valparaíso, the cargo included two live cows which were kept in the dark lower deck. My sons visited the cows every morning and got used to feeding them, and the cows became their pets. They were shocked, however, when after one week of travel they only saw one cow, as the crew had butchered the other one. They were so sad and upset about this incident that they refused to eat meat for the rest of the journey.

---

[10] Due to the extreme isolation of Easter Island back then, its population had no immunity against viruses common on the Continent. The Pascuenses were forbidden to leave the island for fear of contracting infectious diseases, the most common being tuberculosis..

11

From Valparaíso the *Allipén* took a northwest course and during the passage of the Humboldt Current, which took about three days, a cold southern wind caused a chill for the passengers and a continuous rolling of the ship by several degrees to each side. As we navigated away from the continent and began to approach the subtropical region, the climate along with the sea and sky scenery began to change. Large cotton-like cumulus clouds suddenly appeared on the horizon. The dark green tones of the Pacific in the Humboldt Current began turning into a beautiful light blue tint. As we passed into the warmer sea, flying fish began to appear and we came to the realization that we were getting closer to another world.

The climate turned warmer and we began seeing the subtropical rains, both violent and transient and dumping water in a limited space over the ocean. It was fantastic for us to witness for the first time in the subtropics, the movement of a small white cloud along the horizon in the middle of a bright sunny day, to grow little by little and transform into a large dark cloud. Then the cloud would abruptly dump a curtain of water beneath it, like opening up its water faucet. We would later become more familiarized with these tropical showers in Easter Island, where the lack of rivers and creeks made them a blessing from the heavens, in the broadest sense of the word.

Life aboard the ship was passing by with idle tranquility. Conversations and reading would occasionally be interrupted with the anguish caused by our active children, full of curiosity and their nautical explorations throughout the vessel. Our hair would stand on end when our boys would get close to the almost miniature side railings of the *Allipén*, as we could imagine them falling into the ocean.

Our fear turned to real panic the day that, in one of my frequent roll calls, Dario Jr. turned up missing. Our despair grew rapidly and then all of the passengers became concerned; we began a fierce search throughout the ship. We searched over and under stairwells and every corner and all quarters, asking everyone if they had seen him. Our affliction was becoming a terrible anguish, as we had begun to imagine our son drowning at sea. Suddenly out of a hatch Dario appeared, with a mischievous grin and entirely unaware of the presumed tragedy—his reaction was: "What's all the fuss about?". His face was both red and blackened with coal dust after his "inspection review" in the boiler room. In his curiosity for knowing everything on board, he had been running to the far corners of the ship and we did not look down in that area because a seaman had told us he was not there. After this horrific episode, how happy and relieved we were and we hugged him for minutes. We also made clear to our children the discipline that was necessary to ensure their safety for the remainder of the journey.

The officers' mess hall had a large map with a pin attached to a flag. The children would look forward with great interest as the chief mate moved the pin day by day, indicating our position and route we were following on the passage to Easter Island. It was also interesting to witness the daily use of the sextant by the first officer, as he would determine the position of the *Allipén* on the Earth's surface by observing the stars. How slowly we were seeing our advance across that immense Pacific Ocean. It was entertaining for us to hear all the nautical explanations given to us by the skipper: nautical miles, knots, sub-oceanic rocks, currents, and anything else that is superficially known to those in their youth who have read books of Salgari, dreaming about pirates and long sea voyages.

As we were coming to our final night on the ship and grew nearer to the island, our expectations were increasing; would Rapa Nui be similar to the stereotypical Polynesian islands the American cinema had shown us so often with palm trees and extensive white sandy beaches, where girls with leis and sarongs danced melodically to sweet and exotic songs? These questions, along with many others, became our new fantasies and they would soon be answered with the realities upon our arrival.

Eleven days had gone by with nothing in sight but sky and ocean; the *Allipén* appeared to be navigating at a snail's pace, at a mere seven knots. There was great excitement, therefore, when the Captain announced we would arrive the following day on Sunday at eight in the morning and that there would be a farewell dinner that night. The crew set up an attractive arrangement for that dinner under the canopy on the upper deck and at nine P.M. all passengers and officers gathered for the event. The food was delicious and the festive mood touched everyone that night. We toasted to those present as well as those absent and found any other good excuses to drink. Between drinks everyone took turns to toast and after a while the oratory became more flowery, and it was reminiscent of the Roman and Athenian orators Cicero and Demosthenes. Once the speeches ended, singing began and then polyphonic choirs were improvised. Suddenly the Pascuenses joined the group and began singing melodic Polynesian songs. Those sweet songs would later become so familiar to us.

We went to bed quite late that night, and the excitement of being able to begin seeing the island over the horizon at around 4 A.M. made us stay awake that short night. Early at dawn, we were all trying to break through the darkness to see who will spot the island first. We all felt a bit like the seaman aboard Columbus' *Pinta*, Rodrigo de Triana, when he shouted, "Land in sight!"

Who saw the island first? I don't really know, but I remember that all of us were gathered at starboard trying to make sense of an elongated black shadow far into the western horizon.

The East slowly began to show the mild range of colors from dawn break and then the color of the sky would shift slowly from a deep red into a gradually lighter pink and then clear blue. At the same time, looking toward the West, the island's landscape was becoming crisper, and we could begin seeing volcanoes and some steep cliffs. Both sceneries, the East with its dawn and the West with the blurry island, were equally stunning and it was difficult to choose one sight over the other; so the family began running from side to side of the ship in order not to miss anything in this beautiful natural theater stage. This was truly an unforgettable experience. As time passed, the clarity increased and the last few stars gradually disappeared from the sky. Then we saw a red spot at the far East horizon that became a disk that began rising with dignity, making me understand the reverence that the ancient Egyptians had for the nascent Sun, as well as the solar god

Horus who conquered god Seth in the darkness of nights. Despite the numerous clouds which are common in such latitudes, their bright sun rays illuminated the sky and they would appear to get diffused as they traveled away from the Sun. What a spectacle that was!

Soon we saw the island get closer, but what a disappointment when we did not see the thick tropical vegetation that we were expecting. We could see volcanoes, rocks, arid terrain and desolation. And this was the island of our dreams where we would be living for a couple years! I confess I felt an enormous disappointment, which turned into sadness when I saw the expression of Adriana witnessing Rapa Nui for the very first time. Our children, on the other hand, could not contain themselves, and were running around the deck with this vision of an eternal vacation.

As the *Allipén* began circling the island looking for suitable anchorage, we could see high cliffs that resulted from the erosion by waves against the famous Rano Kao Volcano, which is a true landmark at one of the corners of this triangular island. The waves were breaking at its base leaving white foam. The Captain informed us that we would be turning around the volcano cliffs and we would be approaching three islets: Motu Iti, Motu Tautara and Motu Nui. The ship would drop anchor a few miles away from the island in front of the unprotected Hanga Piko bay, which was located adjacent to the village of Hanga Roa, where we would be settling down into our new home. We were also told—to our relief—that the west side of Rapa Nui where we would be living was different, with more vegetation, making it more lively and picturesque.

Indeed, the scenery did change as we were just a few miles from shore and could see the green vegetation. The Rano Kao volcano that has such dramatic landscape from its southeast side acquired a rounded and soft profile from the West. The volcano was also spotted with some trees scattered around its sides. Further down the island we could see the dock at the Hanga Piko bay holding a large crowd of people and surrounded by the beautiful white surf. Turning toward the left it was the village of Hanga Roa, as we could see a multitude of cottages that were surrounded by trees. We could even see the banana trees (new to us) with their bright large green leaves and some small trees called *Miro Tahiti*. Moving our gaze further to the left the scenery was becoming arid again. The landscape was desolate with less vegetation and some black pointy stones gave a macabre character to that area. In the middle of this diverse scenery were many people on the coastline observing us, and others galloping on horseback, apparently overly excited about this annual arrival of a vessel from the mainland.

In addition to these first impressions of the overall island scenery, we could see numerous narrow canoes, appearing very unstable and crowded with dark-skinned and muscular islanders. They were dressed in clean white clothing wearing straw hats, many of which were decorated with feathers—it was all quite colorful. Once the ship's maneuvers to drop anchor were completed, the canoes came to the side of the vessel and the invasion began[11]. With great agility, the islanders began climbing up the side of the ship like spiders, grabbing anything they could with their hands and feet, utilizing any hanging lines from the ship and ladders. A few minutes later the *Allipén* was swarming with muscular male natives bartering their *tolomiros* [12] for our used clothing, shoes, soap—and the most sought after items: sunglasses. With great curiosity we carefully climbed down a ladder alongside the enormous ship into a small dinghy that bounced up and down in the waves. We rode the massive waves around the ship and on to a turbulent two-mile ride to the Hanga Piko pier.

As soon as we stepped on the pier, we found ourselves surrounded by a friendly multitude of children and young people, white clothing contrasting with their dark skin. The barefoot natives were all smiling and touching us, offering us their friendship. They welcomed us in

---

[11] The ship has to anchor a couple miles away, as there is insufficient depth by the dock and there is a barrier of coral reef.

[12] Small wooden carved statues made from *tolomiro* wood, a typical tree from Easter Island. These statues were replicas of moais, *tangata kava kava* (a man with ribs) and *tangata manu* (the bird man). Most Pascuenses had woodcarving skills, which were passed from generation to generation.

a primitive Spanish mixed with Polynesian words. We then began a two-mile walk toward our new house which had been assigned to us in the village of Hanga Roa. The dirt road was lined with stone walls made of *pircas*[13], volcanic rocks gathered from the fields, and banana trees were scattered back near some small houses. We were followed by a large crowd—a true caravan of natives who were looking at us as if we were from another planet, pointing at us, and once in a while touching us with their fingers. Furthermore they were making numerous commentaries that were hard to understand—to the point that our youngest son Gonzalo exclaimed in a loud voice for all to hear: "These Pascuenses are a real pest!"

During our walk toward Hanga Roa, "the metropolis of Rapa Nui," we were met by the mayor of the island, Pedro Atán (the best wood carver in the island and a member of the most prominent family), who gave us the official welcome and invited us for a refreshing pineapple drink in honor of our arrival. It felt so good after the long walk under the burning midday Sun, but the children were anxious to see their new home so we continued down the dusty road.

Our home turned out to be a small rectangular cement house. It had been designed in the shape of a shoe box with a porch leading to the doorway. There were two bedrooms for the six of us, a living and dining room, a bathroom and a kitchen. It also had two additional quarters and a bathroom for live-in maids. There was virtually no furniture and of course no utilities or appliances. The house was surrounded by a garden with vegetation that was somewhat unkempt. In spite of all of this culture shock, we felt very close to our new home in our new habitat and we liked it from that day on. We knew that our household move from the mainland included furniture and a kerosene-powered refrigerator, a unique luxury on the island at that time and very useful for our needs during our stay.

During this first day on the island, even though the boxes from the move had not yet arrived and there was minimum furniture

---

[13] The *pirca* walls are very similar to those used extensively in Ireland.

in each room, it was difficult to walk inside the house because it was full of people everywhere. There were Pascuenses sitting on the few chairs, on the beds and even on the floor. The natives kept inspecting us with inquisitive smiles and making comments that we could not understand—we felt like strange species in a zoo. After they left our house after dark, the Pascuenses kept observing from the outside. My children remember trying to close the curtains when a Pascuense face had its nose against the window looking in at my sons with a welcoming smile. We would learn we would not have much privacy during our stay on Easter Island.

But in perspective, we were on Easter Island, *Rapa Nui*. Our crossing a big portion of the Pacific Ocean to get there had ended, and in a way, we were beginning to become Pascuenses ourselves, islanders in the most isolated place on Earth.

Adriana with her four sons (wearing clothing made at home) with the governor on "Main Street"

Chapter Three

Life and Solitude in Easter Island

Being in the middle of the vastest ocean on Earth and in a place so lonely and far away from any inhabited land with no regular contacts with other places is something that, viewed from the mainland, was simply an intellectual concept; but once in the island that concept became a true feeling of isolation that is very difficult to express in words.

I should recall that at the beginning of the 1950's, the island communicated with the mainland only once a year, by a vessel chartered by the Easter Island Company. Outside of that annual visit, the only other contact with Chile was through the naval radio station. I venture to say that the basic life in the island during the 1950's was not unlike, in many respects, the life that the western world would have experienced several centuries ago. Our stay on Easter Island can thus also be viewed as a journey to the past in a magical time capsule.

There were no public utilities—electricity, running water or telephone—currency was not used, as there were no stores to buy anything. Besides sharing[14], bartering was the trade mechanism to

---

[14] There was no concept of private property as we know it. Goods were to be used and consumed by those who needed them; basically a family approach to "going into the refrigerator".

exchange basic goods, such as foods, clothing, carved statues and other artisan products. The signs of industrialization timidly surfaced by the two motor vehicles on the island: a WW II Jeep and an old farm tractor used to haul trailers with wool for storage and shipping. Besides those two motorized vehicles which were kept for limited use, transportation was limited to walking and horseback riding. There were no bicycles on the island since roads were virtually nonexistent.

Despite the lack of material amenities and creature comforts, there was no perceived poverty. The islanders' nourishment was ample and healthy and they lived with dignity. There was also no crime. It was basically a happy society with an almost childlike demeanor and plenty of ingenuity.

To satisfy the needs of the population, basic supplies were brought by ship and distributed on a welfare system together with rations of lamb meat dispensed each week by the Easter Island Company. The island population was around 800 natives and 40 mainlanders.

Upon our arrival, when approaching the island and seeing it appear after many days of navigation, we were reminded that on the maps it only figured as a speck in the middle of the sea and now we could understand what that really meant, with all of its limitations and smallness. A few days later, when the ship that brought us here returned on a late afternoon and gradually disappeared into the horizon, cutting off any material linkage with the mainland, we felt the isolation and loneliness with more realism, and—why not—with fear.

Once we were settled into our home we all felt less lonely. The warmth of our family with four children filled us with joy with their laughter, surrounded by our books, our little pictures from the mainland, and the vases that decorated our Santiago living room. We even sensed that all of a sudden our parents or some close friend would drop by to visit us. But we had been transplanted to Easter Island and the pleasant reminder was to hear native Pascuense phrases and see many wide and smiling tan faces around us.

Time was passing by and we were getting more used to our little island. The sense of isolation was gradually diminishing through our daily activities: visiting the small and meagerly-supplied hospital, the patients, homeschooling the children, and managing the house, the vegetable garden and the henhouse. We were feeling comfortable with everything that represented our limited and new world.

Little by little we were being mutated into islanders. I took off my suit and tie and exchanged them for short-sleeved shirts and pants and put away my shoes for comfortable espadrilles. Only the rain made me wear thick boots and dress up with a raincoat that every day was getting more difficult to wear. I stopped being the "Doctor" to become the "*Taote*". My wife kept her style and elegance with a casual smart look, appropriate for an informal beach resort: sunhats, light tops, sandals and swimsuits. The kids only wore bib overalls, jeans and swimsuits. It was so wonderful to be able to dress like that!

The day-to-day work was distributed in daily visits to the hospital, weekly visits to the leper colony and home visits to patients, which here were only a few. Adriana focused on the affairs of the house and managed the three live-in maids: one was Laura, a middle-aged lady from the mainland who was an excellent seamstress and was valuable for making and repairing clothing for the family. The other two maids were Pascuenses in their twenties who helped in the cooking and house cleaning and laundry. By dealing with the Pascuense maids Adriana became very proficient in the language. Like any good mother, she loved cooking yummy pastries for tea time[15]. She took care of the vegetable garden and the henhouse; she also shared the duty with me of teaching our sons in the schooling we had established at our home. Our children attended class daily with a strict school schedule and discipline, as education was the first priority. At the same time the boys had time available for horseback riding, swimming in the ocean and playing freely. Upon our arrival we received as gifts several horses, or better said, runt horses, somewhat clumsy, that were easily tamed—even for

---

[15] Chileans are very fond of tea time at about 5 P.M. (known as *"onces"*). It's used as a meal to socialize among family and with guests. Dinners are of course late, at around 9 P.M.

the children. When our third son, Roberto, age 9, would go for a walk, his white horse (Whitie) would follow him like an obedient puppy.

At noon after the morning classes, our family would go to the primitive Hanga Roa dock behind the house for our daily swim in the ocean, which was relaxing and enjoyable for everyone. The warm and transparent ocean was very inviting for an "easy" swim. Its translucent blue color, which allowed you to see the rocky ocean floor and marine life with clarity, invited us to dive and swim. What a difference from the cold ocean of our Chilean coasts!

While there was no beach in Hanga Roa, there was rolling surf some 100 meters from the dock, resulting from the coral reef. Once our children mastered their swimming style, in a few months they turned into real Polynesians, competing successfully against them. They also mastered something that my wife and I could not achieve—the "*ngaru*", a typical Polynesian sport, which was basically body surfing with a light flat board. As surfers do, they would swim far into the ocean and wait patiently for the good big wave to come and as good surfers they learned how to "read the waves" [16]. Once the appropriate wave was selected, they would catch it at its crest and have an exhilarating ride all the way back to the rocky beach. With all this excitement it was a challenge to keep the boys out of the water. Only their starving tummies caused by all the strenuous exercise could motivate them to go back home for lunch.

Adriana, who is a strong swimmer, fell in love with the ocean and she rarely missed a day of swimming. She adapted a swimming style used by the Polynesians, based on the sidestroke. It involved a forward underwater stroke leaning the body to one side and using a scissors kick, in order to minimize effort by being submerged yet sacrificing speed. The problem arose when, one day, Adriana felt overconfident in her swimming abilities. She went swimming alone far out into the ocean and ran into an undercurrent which pulled her far away from shore. Adriana began screaming for help, and fortunately some young Pascuenses heard her from shore and jumped into the ocean to rescue

---

[16] They concluded that the good ones would come every five to seven waves depending on the tide of the day.

her. Their heroic rescue avoided a terrible tragedy, for which I am ever thankful to them.

The four Verdugo brothers, with a Pascuense neighbor
holding a lobster found while swimming

In the afternoons, after the workday, we would go out and enjoy the outdoors. We often would go to the seashore and engage in running and jumping competition with the kids. (At the time I could still beat them.) Other times we had long conversations on diverse topics, which forced us to answer thoughtfully and explain every single issue coming to the children's minds. Many times they put us in a tough situation, asking questions about human reproduction, and the differences between males and females, for example, and we needed to postpone our answers for the following day, after reflection and researching them thoroughly. The diversity of topics that we covered, together with the school lessons that we had to prepare for the following day, kept Adriana and I up late most nights studying, supported only by the tenuous light of a kerosene lamp.

I remember with special affection our occasional excursions, which when accompanied by islanders turned out to be very lively and loud. I particularly evoke an invitation we had for a curanto, also known as *umu*, in the beautiful caves of Hanga Oteo[17]. It was a very hot day and inside the cave it was even hotter as a result of the curanto pit where the food was being cooked. The primitiveness of the setting was accentuated further by the darkness and some bones scattered on the ground. I remember being in my swim shorts chewing a piece of meat from a bone that I was holding with my hands when my wife approached me and whispered in my ear: "Whatever happened to that young and civilized doctor that I married some time ago?"

Other afternoons we used to go to the "movies". On Easter Island we had access to a movie theater with a panoramic screen, glorious Technicolor, air conditioned and a three-dimensional screen. This "Rapa Nui Movie Theater" was the memorable sunsets! We accommodated ourselves in the proper spot with no need of an usher, and the show started once the Sun, approaching the horizon, would dip slowly into the ocean. The sinking Sun set the clouds on fire with deep reddish colors, and then the wind would push them—prompting their rhythmical dances. The cotton-shaped cumulus changed their whiteness into pink, gradually becoming more and more intense. At the same time the stratus formations with their horizontal red lines would cross the sky from end to end. The dark nimbus—like the villains in the movies—varied their dark gray tonalities and pushed by the wind they would swallow up the smaller colorful clouds. Adding to the total scenery up in the sky, the cirrus resembled Monet-like impressionist strokes.

---

[17] *Curanto* is a typical local method from cooking a variety of foods in the ground. The first step is to dig a hole in the ground about a meter and a half deep (approximately 1½ yards). (The area of this hole depends on the number of people.) As a second step, red hot volcanic rocks are placed in the hole.

Next step is to spread a blanket of banana leaves. On these, they place the ingredients: lobster, lamb meat, pork, chicken, sweet potatoes, corn and other vegetables. A new layer of leaves is laid on the ingredients; on top of these, wet sacks to trap the heat. Eveything is then covered with soil, making this a true pressure cooker.

When smoke begins to escape through the soil, it is an indication that it is time to uncover the curanto. The food has been perfectly cooked by the heat of the stones and is moist and delicious, with the various flavors of the ingredients fully blended.

Curanto cooking is also used in southern Chile with somewhat different ingredients.

This was an almost absurd polychrome show, composed of all the figures drawn by the clouds against the colorful sky. Then the characters appeared, according to the spectator's inspiration and imagination, or his or her emotional state of mind. Soon a pirate ship would appear, then a little piglet, and in this paradoxical celestial "tutti-frutti" it was not unusual that at a distance a giant dragon would struggle with an imaginary jet plane crossing by.

The children's vivid imagination was boundless and we all dreamed and enjoyed nature's magnificent displays. Then all of a sudden, with that characteristic which is typical when in proximity to the Equatorial line, the Sun would sink quickly and the night would cover us with its quilt full of bright stars. Living in the city one forgets the aesthetic pleasure of contemplating a starry sky, which turns out to be the most beautiful and incredible show. There was Sirius, the most brilliant star, and Canopus the yellow-white super giant star, from the Carina constellation. Then right in front of us there was the old Southern Cross and *Las Tres Marías*[18], which we considered to be "very Chilean". They were also part of the "Pascuense sky", but with a different inclination from the horizon, and they reminded us of our faraway land. While these thoughts turned us a little melancholy, our boys with their games and laughter would bring us back to happiness.

The nights with a bright moon permitted much more activity outdoors. The islanders would come out with their guitars and fill the surroundings with music. Small groups would gather at the Hotu Matua plaza, a village landmark located in front of the Hanga Roa bay and consisting of a plateau covered by *toroco*—the island grass—at the steps of a towering *moai*. Soon the guitars launched their sweet chords, and afterwards, in tune with the melodic Polynesian songs, the dancers would join rhythmically moving their hips and shoulders...the nights were filled with mystery.

---

[18] These three stars which are part of Orion's Belt are normally called "The Three Kings" (or "The Magi"). In some places such as South America, they are known as "Las Tres Marias" or "As Três Marías" (The Three Marys)..

On Sundays we all went together to the mass offered by the priest, Fr. Sebastian Englert. The mass liturgy was of course identical to the one on the mainland, but everything else was so different. Especially at the beginning, everything seemed very foreign to all of us. For an unknown moral reason, there was a sharp gender split at mass: the men sat in the pews left of the aisle, while the women in the pews on the right side. The songs were vibrant and all participated enthusiastically with beautiful Polynesian themes. When going to Communion, under sounds of the loud choir, the islanders walk with a rhythm reminiscent of the southern seas. The sermon was delivered in Pascuense, by Fr. Englert who dominated it, but of course, it left us pretty much in the dark.

Pascuense is the native language in Easter Island; it is a Polynesian dialect derived from Tahiti. Since the language is simple, focusing mainly on objects and adjectives, it is a challenge to express more abstract thoughts. When Father Sebastian explained that Christians' lives were under the guidance of Christ he would simply say: we are all under God's "*Cahuja*" which means butt…and they understood this concept clearly.

As we approached our second year in the island, I decided to become an amateur radio operator to be able to communicate with our family back in Santiago, so I ordered the equipment from Chile for the next annual shipment. I was proudly granted a ham radio operator's license—my ID was CE-0-AC and I had cards printed with a *moai* which became very desirable[19]. The Navy base on the island lent me a small electrical generator and some fuel, which allowed me to use the radio equipment on limited occasions. After overcoming many difficulties, especially with setting up the electric power with the generator (for which my son Pedro was the 'expert mechanic') and the installation of the antenna supported by a tall mast erected

---

[19] When ham operators connect they mail each other postcards, called "QSL cards," with the ID and an icon representative of their places. The Easter Island card was truly unique.

by my children, I was able to make it work. To my surprise however, a couple of days after the proud launch of our radio station the Naval Governor showed up at my home with his lieutenant to order me to lower the height of the antenna. In his view it was inappropriate to have a structure on the island that would be higher than the tallest mast where the Chilean flag flew at the Governor's house. I was unsuccessful in convincing him that I was not being disrespectful to the Chilean flag, nor was I challenging the Chilean sovereign or his authority over the island; I even suggested flying the Chilean flag on our antenna.

As a result of this unsuccessful negotiation with the Governor, we ended up lowering the antenna a few feet after making careful measurements. While it was a good engineering lesson for my four sons, I suspect that it degraded the capability of my ham radio equipment, which needed all the help it could get to reach far away distances. (But Pedro did end up studying engineering.)

I was disappointed to realize that in spite of all my effort to connect with Chile, it was either very difficult, or simply impossible. The first and one of the few times that I could talk with my parents I was so overwhelmed by emotions that my words drowned in my throat. A different story was with the U.S., especially California, where I was able to establish many contacts. When I turned on the equipment and started calling[20], many ham operators tried to reach me, since it was very unique to contact someone from a place so remote and exotic. The reality is that the ham equipment became more of an entertainment and not the tool that I had envisioned for connecting with our loved ones back in Chile.

Having a ham radio as our entertainment, we decided that it would be nice to share some of the music that we could receive from far away stations with the Pascuenses, so we organized occasional musical gatherings by placing speakers in front of our porch. We had just paved the 100-foot walkway from the gate entrance to the front porch. Many

---

[20] As a ham operator the general call was made by saying: "CQ-10, this is CE 0 AC" calling, and people hearing somewhere in the world would get very excited to reach us.

Pascuenses came that first Sunday afternoon for our get-together. While they enjoyed the music, especially German marches that they had heard during warship visits during WWII, they were most impressed by the paved walkway. They had never seen such "soft large flat rock", and since most of them didn't wear shoes it was a pleasure just to walk on the cement—to the point of asking if they could come back some other day with their families for a promenade. We were not accustomed to having much privacy in the island and we knew it was a real treat for the many Pascuenses who returned several times with their families for a back and forth stroll on our walkway. With these real live examples in a simple life we realized how little it takes to achieve pleasure from material comforts, and as we get more and more we desire more in a never ending progressive chain of material desires leading eventually to greed in extreme cases.

I have to make a special mention of the eating habits we had to get used to during our stay in the island. The annual event of the vessel visit to the island left very basic staples at the island's commissary, such as sugar, flour, noodles, rice and legumes (mainly dried beans). Unfortunately, after some six months from arrival the sugar would spoil from the excessive humidity, and the rest of the food would attract a diversity of bugs, making them unsuitable for eating; so we had to be creative with our menus during the second half of the year. Fortunately our vegetable garden provided us with tasty produce. We also enjoyed the bananas, sweet potatoes, pineapples, figs and juicy and tasty oranges. The main source of animal protein came from fish, lobster—abundant in Easter Island—and lamb, which was distributed by the Easter Island Company to everyone on a weekly basis free of charge. We ate so much lamb that we joked about it making our voices sound "lamb-like". We actually enjoyed this meat since the mutton on Easter Island has a low fat content and my wife cooked it magnificently well—as with everything she does. We also relied on the chicken and fresh eggs from our henhouse at the back of our one-hectare (2½ acre) property. We would occasionally enjoy pork chops when sacrificing a pig, which created an occasion in which dozens of islanders would gather at our house. Among all these foods, we could identify closest to the sweet potato, or *"kumara"*. When the flour turned spoiled with bugs and we could no longer bake bread, the *kumara* became an excellent substitute. It may appear strange, but a cup of coffee accompanied with *kumara* became a habit and a delicious breakfast for us.

The chicken coop was my wife's pride and joy, and she took care of it daily, aided by the children, especially when collecting the eggs. In spite of all this special care, an infectious bird flu struck the coop and killed many of the chickens. As the chickens became ill they started to lower their wings when walking, and after a few days they would die. Our kids associated the chickens dragging their wings with Count Dracula, wearing his long black cape. Therefore, when a chicken got infected and started to drag its wings, the kids labeled that condition as *"draculismo"*, which turned into a synonym for being sick. That expression has survived over the years in our family, and when someone shows signs of sickness we refer to such condition as *"draculismo"*.

When talking about food and our henhouse, I cannot forget one anecdote of a medicine-nurturing type. Eager to improve the yield from our "barn", I decided to transform some of the chickens into capons, and I took the initiative to "operate" on some of them. I designated my wife as the nurse assistant and I acted as the anesthetist and surgeon. Unfortunately, due to my lack of experience in administering anesthesia to birds, I applied too much ether to my first "chicken patient" and the poor bird died on me during surgery. Later, a visitor dropped by to have lunch with us, and Adriana thought that it would be a great idea to prepare the chicken that had abruptly passed away. So the deceased chicken got quickly transferred from the operating table to the kitchen table. When Adriana served the stew, it looked very appetizing, but when we tasted it we noticed a terrible ether flavor, but no one dared to say a thing so we all ate in silence. After our guest left, my wife and I speculated about his likely comments on the lunch he had just had. Perhaps he thought the flavors of all meals at our home were influenced by the Greek god Galen and my medical profession. He, of course, never came back to visit us again during meal times.

A serious challenge on the island was the scarcity of drinking water, which was solved by gathering the rainwater that fell on the roof of the house and collected through the gutter with pipes draining into a cement tank built next to the back of our house. That water was used for drinking, cooking and bathing for the six of us.

I must describe the nature of this "precious water". It was basically clean water, as it drained from a master pipe installed at the lower part of the tank but a few inches from the bottom. One day I decided to climb up to inspect the tank, and to my surprise I saw all kinds of residue and little stones on the bottom, while the surface was covered by dead floating cockroaches and dry leaves. I realized that trying to remove impurities would simply mix them with the water, and so it was best left untouched. We rationalized that the water draining from the middle of the tank was therefore clean. We never got sick drinking that water and it had a very fresh taste.

When experiencing droughts it was frustrating to see on the horizon some rainy-looking clouds approach our house and then pass by our heads without leaving us with a single drop of rain. Then the clouds would suddenly drop a curtain of water as they moved over the ocean while we watched with frustration. Other times the clouds would indeed give us their gift of water on the roof of our house and we would all celebrate. There is no doubt that water was a gift from the heavens.

Illuminating the house at night was another challenge. We had to get used to candles and kerosene lamps for lighting, which we could deal with in most cases. However, when we had to study long hours at night to prepare the lessons for our children the next day, we really missed good lighting.

Among the most positive experiences of our wonderful stay in Easter Island was the absence of money[21]. I could forget about

---

[21] In the 1950's the Chilean economy was experiencing hyperinflation accompanied by price controls and rationing of basic goods. This condition which lasted for many years created enormous anxiety and strong distaste for anything associated with economy and currency.

my wallet and my wife did not have to carry her purse. That was a gratifying experience; the invention of currency by the Phoenicians had not contaminated the island with its aftermath of ambition, social class divisions (which are mainly driven by monetary wealth), and all the tricks to earn it and increase it, etc. Without a doubt, that aspect of life on Easter Island still belonged to the Eden of our ancestors. That is how our lifestyle developed while in Easter Island: simple, primitive and without the complications and conventionalism of the "civilized" world.

I remember two occasions during our stay in the island when I felt the oppression of loneliness and solitude—almost physically. The first time was when I had to get up in the middle of the night to visit a very sick patient at his home, about a month after our arrival. I left home and walked along the "main street" (at that time it was the only street), which consisted of a road bordered by low *pirca* walls, small cottages, banana trees and *miro tahitis*, the most common trees of the island at that time. It was pitch black, with a crystal clear sky, one that you can only find in the middle of the ocean and on Easter Island. The darkness was so intense that the stars illuminated my walk. I found myself surrounded by dormant volcanoes, and the shadows cast from the trees looked like ghosts. I could hear the sound of the ocean as the surf crashed. I started to feel a sensation of loneliness that made me extremely anxious. Honestly, I was scared. It was a cosmic solitude. I felt alone in the beginnings of the world, in the middle of the universe...alone, alone, completely alone...I kept walking and—with a great effort and praying to God—I overcame that feeling and I was able to visit my patient with a more calmed soul after that intense experience of solitude.

The other occasion when I felt that sensation of intense loneliness and isolation was one afternoon, when I climbed for the first time up the Maonga Terevaka, the island's highest mountain. From its summit I could see ocean in every direction—360°, like standing on the bridge of a ship in the middle of the ocean. I could see the water joining the horizon in a line that visualizes the curvature of the Earth. From the summit of this arid and rocky mountain, one has the impression of being in the middle of nowhere. With that sight I experienced a sensation of anxiety, different from my feelings of that dark night, but it was a real sense of solitude as well.

Besides these two isolating occasions on the island, only in rare circumstances did I experience true solitude and nostalgia. When those feelings overwhelmed me, I fought actively to distance myself from them, knowing that it could be serious to have them penetrate one's soul, while the reality was that we had been transplanted to a place where there is no possibility to neutralize its underlying causes: distance and isolation.

The Verdugo family on their porch with a Navy officer

CHAPTER FOUR

INTERLUDE: REFLECTIONS OF A MOAI

I have been silent on this rocky ledge for such a long time without saying a single word that I have decided to speak up today to relate my earlier years and share my thoughts of what I have seen and heard during my many centuries of life.

Here I stand with my large family totaling over one hundred brother moais on the slopes of the Rano Raraku volcano with our backs to the sea. Most of my siblings and I were born in the quarry of this volcano, and live in silence and isolated from the world. We were erected some 500 years ago, soon after Christopher Columbus crossed the Atlantic to the new world. I understand that we have become the icon of Easter Island which is recognized all over the world today.

I hear that the first men who arrived at this land and carved us out of volcanic rock were coming from a place called "Hiva,"[22] after escaping from a great cataclysm. The first settlers were being commanded by their king Hotu Matua who wanted to save his people from that catastrophe. The legend says that king Hotu Matua navigated in two large primitive vessels loaded up with fern plants, sandalwood trees, rushes, moss, banana shoots, taro seedlings, sugarcane, yam, sweet potatoes, yellow roots, *tolomiro* plants, working tools, along with birds, pigs, and chickens. The king brought along his wife, Vaka A Hiva, his brother Oroi and his sister Ava Rei Púa, plus some 400 of his subjects. Today, the natives still remember them all in the lyrics of their native Polynesian songs.

Following a long journey, the settlers landed on the Anakena beach and the new land was baptized as *Te Pito O Te Henua* (the "belly button of the world"). It should be pointed out that in that period the island was covered by trees and a wide variety of vegetation, including giant palm trees (a fact which was only recently re-discovered by paleontologists).

Hotu Matua, who is always alive in the memories and traditions of the island, was a wise and honorable leader who distributed the land equitably among his people. Following their arrival he taught them

---

[22] "Hiva" is referred to as a generic mainland

many skills, including construction of lodging and cultivation of the land. The king was also keen on culture and art and he instructed his wise men to transfer extensive hieroglyphic writings onto wooden tablets which they had brought with them from Hiva in rolls of banana leaves. Those early carved wooden tablets constituted the first *rongo rongo*s, which could only be understood and deciphered by a few wise men who were considered to be the intellectual elite. From this same time period the first sculptures of us were made in a somewhat crude form, contrasting with the refined elegance that we later moais possess and of which we are all very proud. The more primitive moais were erected to pay tribute to and memorialize certain members of society after their death. The moais were erected on top of the *ahus*—platforms of stacked-up stone which were funerary monuments. The funeral of the important members of society, such as *tangata manu* (military chiefs), were conducted in the *ahu*s. People of lower social categories were buried under simple stones constructed on a semi-pyramid shape—basically small burial mounds.

I am aware of the incredible precision in the fit of the stones in these *ahu*s. I was informed by the numerous conversations that I overheard from Thor Heyerdahl, a Norwegian archeologist who visited us, in the comparative research made with the Inca monuments of Peru, especially in the Machu Picchu area. After seeing comparable stone fittings in both places located so far away from each other, Heyerdahl formulated the hypothesis that the first inhabitants could have come from the Peruvian coast of South America.

It appears that in the beginning, the islanders were organized into two tribes—the Hotuitis, who were dedicated to farming the land, and the Tu'uaros, who were fishermen. They lived peacefully in a society that enjoyed an abundance of food. As years went by within this comfortable lifestyle, the population grew substantially larger.

During this early period dwellings were built in the shape of an inverted boat, typically Polynesian, called hare paenga. These dwellings consisted of stones which outlined the floor and formed the foundation normally placed between rocks and sand. Curved depressions in the stones indicate today where supporting walls once stood. There were other larger constructions built upon the bedrock in which they carved indentations to fit the logs to sustain the roof made from straw mats called *totora*. In addition to these better-known dwellings there were various small ones shaped like primitive huts which were called *tupas*, possibly for use by the lower class.

In the crater's rim of the Rano Kao volcano lies the most impressive Orongo village. I hear that the view from there is stunning: with the breathtaking crater on one side in which one can see the enormous cavity with colorful lagoons at the bottom, to the other side where one sees the crater wall dropping vertically some 1,000 feet to the ocean where the three famous islets are located[23]. The Orongo dwellings have a low height and are made from large flat rocks which are carved with hundreds of petroglyphs depicting the well-known *Tangata Manu* (Bird Man). This village was only used on the eve of the election of the new chief, also called *Tangata Manu*. Inside those dwellings they awaited the arrival of *manu tara* birds, or "Lucky Birds". When the *manu taras* arrived, they set up nests and laid their eggs in the three islets. Each year there was an arduous ritual competition to select a new *tangata manu* chief. The candidates for such an honorable and prestigious nomination would have to scale down the sheer steep cliffs of the Rano Kao volcano, dive into the rough ocean in the middle of the exploding breaking waves against the cliffs, and swim to the nearest tiny islet of Motu Nui where they had to locate and carefully retrieve a *manu tara* egg. With the egg in hand, and totally intact, the candidates for *tangata manu* had to swim back to the cliffs through the rough sea and climb back over the cliffs of the Rano Kao volcano to the Orongo village with the unbroken egg. The winner of the competition was named *Tangata Manu* and he was conferred in a ceremony with special rights and privileges in the community which were granted to him for the duration of the following year.

---

[23] The three islets are described at the arrival of Dr. Verdugo's family on the island: Motu Iti, Motu Tautara and Motu Nui. (See Chapter 2.)

These initial settlers were different than the Pascuenses of today. They had a lighter complexion with very fine facial features. These settlers had a simple life with an economy based on fishing and agriculture. They would worship their deceased ancestors; they would expose them first to the sun rays—their god—on top of the *ahu*s and then bury them inside the *ahu*s. These settlers would carve on the *rongo rongo* tablets strange hieroglyphic characters expressing perhaps long spiritual recitations.

The men carved instruments, weapons and fish hooks out of obsidian, the only volcanic rock-based glass on the island. No one has been able to explain why there was such a feverish obsession to build so many of us moais and our corresponding *ahu*s. It was not an easy task. In addition to carving us, there was the need to carry us from our birthplace in the volcano to various locations throughout the island—a tough task since the wheel was not known then and we tend to be heavy, each one of us weighing in excess of a ton. This might partially explain why the early settlers' energies were channeled into making hundreds of statues and monuments with no time for conflict and, thus, why life was benign and peaceful. The design, construction and transportation of moais needed plenty of resources, which tend to be limited in any society: workers, plenty of food to nourish them well so they could undertake such hard physical tasks, logs to transport us and use as leverage for lifting us up on our ledges. The strong ropes to pull us out to our destinations on the island were made from fiber material from the island trees, and the logs were made from palm trees. With all this hectic construction activity there was overuse of our natural resources; palm trees and arboreal species were cut down without replanting them, and our island's vegetation tragically diminished over time. This unrestricted exploitation of our island's natural resources caused total devastation and extinction of many plant and arboreal species on our beloved island.

The environmental degradation continued and the life of the islanders was slowly unraveling, when one day they spotted a few black dots on the horizon—toward the West where the Sun sets—the black dots grew larger and larger as they got closer and closer to the island. When they slowly approached the coastline, they could see dozens of wide canoes with a different design than those the islanders were familiar with.

The vessels were strange elongated double-hulled voyaging canoes which had nothing in common with the single-hull canoes that were used to navigate from where the Sun rises (East). These canoes came from the opposite direction (West). These newcomers had a robust build, broad backs and shoulders, and not very tall—not as tall as the first settlers that arrived on the island with Hotu Matua. Their skin was tan, their lips thicker and their noses were wider. Their eyes were somewhat elongated, shaped like almonds. Furthermore, their ears were long and perforated at the bottom. They had an unusual custom—men as well as women—to perforate their earlobes and put weights in them in order to elongate their ears. They called them *Hanau Eepe* (long ears) in contrast to the original inhabitants of the island who became known as *Hanau Momoko* (short ears).

From the time these two cultures met there was distrust. To the original inhabitants, the new visitors were intruders who had come to alter the idyllic lifestyle on the island. The new arrivals were themselves running away from cataclysm and wars in western Polynesia—and after a long and stormy journey in the vast Pacific Ocean the new visitors had hoped to have reached their promised land. To their surprise this new frontier was already colonized by another group.

The arrival of this new wave of settlers exacerbated the deforestation, causing further erosion of the fertile soil. As time passed, these conditions led to a severe famine among the expanded population of the island. Gradually diminishing natural resources coupled with unrestrained population growth within any limited space, such as Rapa Nui, represents an explosive combination that leads eventually to calamity and possibly extinction of any society on this planet.

Soon, peace ceased to reign among the feuding cultures, and the struggle for dominance stained the island with blood. The original settlers experienced the worse setback, who in their long years of a peaceful existence, dedicated to a joyful life constructing monuments and carving out petroglyphs, had never been involved in warfare. They were at a disadvantage versus the new invaders, who were experienced in combat and the martial arts that were needed for their survival—their ferocity did not even stop at cannibalism.

As the years went by with many tribal confrontations, the original Short-Ear island inhabitants began to experience casualties in large numbers while the newcomers only suffered minor losses, and became the dominant group of the island.

The demographics and racial profile of the population had been fundamentally altered. The light skin, long noses and thin lips of the original settlers began to fade, and over generations they were replaced by the more crude features of the "Long Ears." Only very few families of the island were able to preserve the pure features of the original inhabitants.

There was overall decadence; after so many years of struggles and destruction the arts and cultural life of the old inhabitants were gradually diminished. Resources were becoming scarce and there was an endless state of hostility—which was not conducive to creative thinking in such a relatively small land. So the islanders no longer created more *ahu*s nor erected more moais to accompany us.

This was the way we witnessed the extinguishing of an advanced culture by barbarians coming from the West. But as new generations produced a new blended society, the behavior of the islanders mellowed, and they became more civilized. In this new tranquil era, the island acquired a new name in addition to its indigenous name, Te Pito O Te Henua: Rapa Nui (Big Island). This new name was in reference to another smaller Polynesian island named Rapa Iti (Little Island), known to the invaders, and which has many similarities to our island.

Following this long consolidation period, a new type of visitor was to alter their life once more. One morning, the islanders saw on the vast emptiness of the ocean something strange. This time there were not dozens of approaching black dots that showed up on the horizon as in the past, but instead three tall vessels that advanced very rapidly from the East. As the vessels got closer, they appeared to grow taller and they were like approaching giants compared to the canoes of the invaders that came from the West so many years ago.

They were three large vessels with enormous sails and a crew of white bearded men, dressed in strange attire covered with shiny armor. This was the Easter morning in the year of 1722, under the command of the Dutch Captain Roggeveen, who baptized the island with its Western name of "Easter Island". The islanders resented enormously that their island had been renamed by foreign aliens, when the native name, "Rapa Nui", already existed for them.

And once they stepped on shore, how strange these aliens looked with their shiny and stiff clothing! How peculiar were the objects they were carrying! But no, they were not peculiar; they were terrible and dangerous objects! They were carrying instruments that sounded like thunder, and the islanders saw that the aliens could cause death at a distance, as the islanders witnessed with horror when one of the Dutch seamen began shooting. The peculiar looking aliens were well received, but with fear—the natives offered them their food and their women, and after staying a few days the aliens continued on their journey West.

I hear from historians that the discovery of Rapa Nui by Westerners was very significant because it brought the end of the Stone Age civilization on the island. From what I understand, it is difficult for Westerners to comprehend the fact that this was the last bastion of the Stone Age, which had lingered for over 3,000 years after the rest of the world had moved on.

Since then, "Easter Island" was placed on the map and navigation charts, opening the way for similar vessels to visit our island from time to time, albeit between long intervals. All of these tall ships appeared to carry similar crews. Two Spanish vessels commandeered by Don Felipe Gonzalez came to the island in 1770. Subsequently, the British Captain Cook reported having been received by very few islanders, most of whom were terribly impoverished: Famine and scarcity had exacted its toll on the population.

A few years later, in 1786, the French Captain LaPérouse came to the island on a goodwill mission, which was designed to improve the living conditions of its people. He brought livestock, including sheep and pigs, and a variety of seeds. LaPérouse's idea was to develop an animal stock through reproduction and to plant vegetable gardens. Unfortunately, the island's culture lacked the notion of investing for the future—and all the livestock and gardens were rapidly eaten by the starving islanders. Other ships also arrived and would anchor for a few days, and some had a crew with well-intentioned men, while others brought evil people with them. A few would leave seeds of life with brief loves, while others left death with their weapons.

A disgraceful incident occurred during 1862, when a pirate flotilla of eight Peruvian vessels came ashore and captured hundreds of islanders against their will to force them to work as slaves in the Guano Islands of Peru. Most of the islanders ended up dying of infectious diseases and starvation, and this caused a severe breakdown in the culture of Rapa Nui, as the wise men who could interpret the *rongo rongo* tablets were taken away as well. After that shameful and devastating desecration, the island population shrank severely to a mere 100 inhabitants.

One of many fallen moais on the island, with restored moais in

41

background at Ahu Tongariki. Photo: Michael Wozniak

On a later occasion a vessel approached the island with a crew who acted very differently than the visitors from prior ships. A few men came ashore, only to return almost immediately to the ship, leaving behind a middle-aged man dressed with long black attire, a few tools and some strange objects that I was told were books. This lonely man neither planted seeds of life nor caused death in the island, but rather, he tried to get close to everyone with a desire to understand and to be understood by the people. At the beginning, the islanders looked at him with disdain and even hostility. But when after a few months the islanders began to accept him and trust him, the same vessel returned to take him away. This endeared visitor was Brother Eugenio Eyraud, who came from the Congregation of the Sacred Heart in the year 1864. Years later Brother Eugenio returned to the island to stay for the rest of his life. This man did not fit the image created by others who had come from the mainland before him. He was neither ambitious nor sensual, he was not seeking material comforts nor was he trying to take advantage of others. He simply preached the gospel and taught a new doctrine of peace and love that he claimed prevailed in the distant land from where he came. Unlike most men who had visited the island in prior journeys, Brother Eugenio indeed practiced what he preached. The islanders began gradually embracing this new doctrine and promoting it among their society; they directed their vision to a single God and they departed from their evil spirits—the *tatanes* and *Make Make*. They embraced Christian values and became better Christians in many ways than those coming from the mainland. The islanders became compassionate and developed love for each other. At times were they promiscuous? They were basically responding to a natural instinct for the reproduction of the human species. In their love there was neither malice nor perversion. Weren't those from the mainland worse? Soon they were baptized and their tranquil, sensual life was touched by the Holy Spirit through Brother Eugenio, and they became better human beings, living in harmony in a more orderly society.

A few years later, in 1870 I hear, a vessel flying a red, white and blue flag with a lonely star showed up from which many young, highly disciplined crewmen came ashore. It was the battleship O'Higgins from the Chilean Navy, conducting the annual training cruise for the midshipmen. Five years later the same vessel returned bringing along among its crew Lieutenant Policarpo Toro, who became very interested in such an isolated territory. Policarpo Toro returned again in 1886, this time commanding the Chilean Navy training ship *Abtao*. Upon the completion of this trip he prepared a formal proposal to the highest Chilean authorities to make our island Chilean territory. With much vision, President Balamaceda approved the proposal and commissioned now-Captain Toro to implement this initiative, by traveling to Tahiti in 1887 to negotiate the proper arrangements with the French Government. He negotiated the acquisition of the island from Tahiti, the legal owner of Easter Island at the time. Then as commander of the *Abtao*, he took possession of Easter Island on behalf of the Chilean Government on September 9, 1888. Since that time, Chile has exercised sovereignty over the island; it has maintained a presence, established control and formulated development plans. These plans were guided by diverse policies not always adequate, but always formulated with good intentions aimed at improving the quality of life for the islanders.

After these long years of remembrance, I have several comments which I have reflected on in solitude, and today I have decided to express them and speak out:

- Why do the bearded men claim that they discovered the island, when it had not only been discovered earlier, but had been populated by highly skilled and educated navigators?

- Why was it renamed "Easter Island", when it already had a musical Polynesian name of "Te Pito O Te Henua" and later "Rapa Nui"?

- Why has there been so much effort to transplant customs and regulations that may be appropriate in the mainland, but may not reflect the lifestyle and culture of the islanders?

There is another terrible uncertainty that concerns me to which I already made an early reference but I wish to reemphasize again: I've learned that when the first inhabitants arrived, the place was a true Garden of Eden covered by vegetation and trees. The few people who arrived eventually multiplied themselves into the thousands, and as centuries passed by, trees were cut to lift and transport us moais, rain and wind eroded the earth without trees and limited vegetation, and then food became scarce. The society was divided not only between the Short Ears, *Hanau Eepe*, and the Long Ears, *Hanau Momoko*, but also among sculptors and priests on the one hand, and the fishermen and farmers on the other. These divisions combined with food shortages caused a crumbling of the social order and an overall anarchy undermining the privileges of the educated elite, the sculptors and priests. The masses had taken over! The majority of the population died and many were eaten through the cannibalism that developed as a result of the prevailing hunger. Following these episodes, another culture developed that, without an elite class who had knowledge and leadership skills, did not flourish and they no longer made more statues that could keep me company nor the monuments nor funeral mounds. The overpopulation and the unrestricted exploitation of natural resources had devastated nature and caused genocide. Isn't this a warning and lesson from God not to destroy the environment of our planet Earth and not to allow an explosive population growth? These thoughts worry me—and how I would like to make them well known so such an insane situation does not develop on a large scale for this planet Earth, which itself is a remote island when compared to the vast universe!

There is another concern that obsesses me. The constant arrival of more people from the mainland bringing to our island their customs and culture:

- Would that erode our idyllic peace, our simple life, or the permanent contact with nature to enjoy sunsets and nights full of stars, which I hear you no longer see in the large cities of this world?

- Would alcohol and drugs arrive? Would horses be replaced by noisy motorcycles and motor vehicles, which I hear has happened on the mainland?

- Would there be a stratification of social classes in the island, in other words separating the rich from the poor?

There are many such questions that I pose. I hope these grave concerns are simply a byproduct of my imagination and not a true reality. I am accustomed to lying quietly by the soft slopes of the Rano Raraku volcano where we still experience nights full of stars, and when the Sun sets in the West, it lightens the clouds hanging over the Pacific Ocean with gorgeous reddish colors as it has been doing continuously for thousands of years.

Chapter Five

A Home Schooling Experience

One of the most challenging problems we had to face in Easter Island was the education of our children. We had the obligation to ensure their education would not suffer as a result of this experience and we felt compelled to refute the many skeptical views from relatives and friends who were predicting failure—that our sons would turn wild and that it would be irresponsible for us to leave Santiago at this stage in our lives. Adriana and I made a strong commitment that we would deal with the boys' education and academic requirements in the best possible way and in no way would we compromise their intellectual development and social behavior.

Education was a key issue that needed resolution, among the numerous and pressing matters that we had to resolve in the limited time available between our decision to leave and our departure from the mainland. First of all, we needed the complete school programs and syllabus for the first cycle of Humanities[24]. A very effective and caring

---

[24] In the Chilean educational system, the Humanities referred to grades 7 through 12 and the curriculum was highly regulated and standardized by the Ministry of Education. The First cycle corresponded to grades 7 through 9. Upon return the children had to validate their studies with formal exams given by teachers appointed by the Ministry of Education.

lady from the Ministry of Education made ample guideline materials available to us within a few days. Next we had to purchase textbooks, reference material and the various school supplies. Since it was the end of the school year,[25] we had difficulty finding such material in the regular bookstores. We even searched in the working-class neighborhood of San Diego—and it was there, among the many used bookstores, that we were rewarded with an old yet very complete Historical Atlas which included beautifully detailed maps. It was a journey through time that covered maps from classic Greece and Rome up to World War I, passing through the invasion of the barbarians, the Napoleonic wars, etc. This old atlas assisted us greatly in teaching our sons their school curriculum.

We arrived on Easter Island in mid-December. We had the summer vacation months ahead of us to organize and put together our ambitious educational project: the *"Liceo Pascuense"*.

The first problem was logistical: where would the school operate? Fortunately we quickly found the solution. A few yards behind our home we had constructed a two-room schoolhouse, which was given to us from a limited supply of wood-frame prefabricated structures that the Chilean Navy had in its local warehouse. This small house had a large window that faced the West, and had the beautiful ocean as its background. It was the perfect setting to hold our classes. It was large, well lit and ventilated. We installed a blackboard on the wall and next to it we hung several maps. Further back was a bookshelf for the schoolbooks with spaces assigned to each one of the boys. We found local island carpenters, who made somewhat rustic but adequate benches and desks. We were all ready to begin the school year in late March, just as on the mainland.

The more difficult part came later: distributing the assignments, determining the schedule and fitting in all the lessons without taking time away from my medical duties. We also had the fortune of relying on the collaboration of Lorenzo Baeza, the primary teacher assigned

---

[25] The school year in Chile ends in December—in the Southern Hemisphere this is the beginning of summer.

from the Ministry of Education to the public school for the natives in Hanga Roa. He offered to teach the curriculum for the history of Chile, as well as shop class. Mr. Baeza also contributed to the enlargement of our student body by enrolling his son, Enrique, who was the same age as Roberto, as an additional student, bringing the total student body to five, ranging in age from 9 through 13. My wife, who had an accounting degree and was skillful in math, covered arithmetic, algebra, and basic French. My faculty responsibilities were focused in science, geometry, Spanish, world history, geography, and English. We began our *Liceo Pascuense* on March 17, 1953, with love, dedication, discipline and consistent education for our sons covering almost two school years.

There were two more challenges that we faced at the *Liceo Pascuense*. The first being the question of how we would group the children in different courses while making the maximum use of the teacher's hours. We resolved this by arranging the children in two groups. The two older boys were placed in the second grade of Humanities, while the two younger ones and Enrique, were placed in the first. We also decided that some classes—languages, arithmetic, history, and geography—would be taught to all five students together, but of these classes some would be educated only during the first half, expanding the second half to my two older sons while the younger students played.

A reality that we had to face was that neither Adriana nor I had any formal tutoring education, and we had to brush up on the specific subjects to be covered. We therefore undertook a major initiative to extensively study and review a wide range of subjects extending from Linnaeus's classification of plants, through the various teeth of mammals, the habits of spiders, Spanish grammar, the Punic Wars, the consequences of the Crusades, and algebra and geometry topics such as the famous Pythagorean Theorem of right triangles, etc. Often we stayed up late until two or three in the morning with the help of a muted candlelight or a kerosene lamp, knowing that we had to be prepared for 8 o'clock sharp when classes began. We made these sacrifices because we felt that as parents and teachers we had to give the children an example of punctuality and strong preparation.

From the first day of school I brought a "book of classes" to register each session taught to the boys and the material that was covered. After so many years have gone by, when my wife and I read over this book of classes, it is impossible for us to express the emotions and nostalgia teaching our sons in Easter Island. Many of the entries also included notes and our lesson plans. I would periodically give tests and assign grades. I not only corrected the exams to see the progression of our students, but also observed the ingenuity of their replies. I recall an occasion when on a quiz I asked for the biological differences between birds and mammals, which we had covered at depth in several sessions, our third youngest son Roberto simply wrote: "birds sleep on a branch while mammals sleep on the ground".

During the second school year in the island, the school's enrollment expanded further to six students by receiving an eleven-year old girl. She was the daughter of an Army officer who had arrived as part of the new military mission to manage for the first time the drafting of young males on the island. Co-ed education was uncommon in Chile at that time, so this constituted a new experience for our boys, and gave them a new perspective on school socialization. We successfully converted the *Liceo Pascuense* into a co-ed school.

The arrival of the Army Mission had a noticeable impact on the island. Its task was to bring Chilean values and symbols to the community to create a sense of national unity. The young island men were drafted as conscripts into barracks for three days per week, where they were given standardized crew cuts, outfitted in rather large-fitting uniforms. The islanders had to get accustomed to wearing boots, which for most of them was the first time they had worn any kind of footwear. The conscripts were taught Chilean history, civic education and martial arts. The Army—which was modeled on the Prussian army—standardized their appearance and behavior in a way that made them lose their Polynesian identity, at least temporarily. The conscripted islanders would look peculiar marching in unison in the Plaza Hotu Matua under the shouted orders from the Chilean sergeant. These weekly marches became new entertainment to the islanders and my children.

A significant event occurred when the Inspector of Education for the Province of Valparaíso, which had jurisdiction over Easter Island, was sent on an official mission in August of 1953, when the SS *Angamos* from the Chilean Navy visited Easter Island. Mr. Héctor Poblete Cabezas' duties were to inspect the public school which offered primary education to the natives. Once he completed his official functions, we requested that he visit our *Liceo,* which he happily agreed to. One morning he honored us by attending some of our classes, posing questions of the children, looking through their notebooks, reviewing their books, etc. He seemed very pleased, but we would have never thought that he would write an official document highly complementary of our *Liceo.* We were most surprised and delighted when, six months later, we received a copy of his report with the next vessel visit. This official document, issued by the Ministry of Education of Chile, was testimony to our educational efforts and results.

Subject: Protocol of Official Educational Review

Easter Island, Hanga Roa, August 11, 1953

As of today I have visited the Secondary[26] study group formed by the children of Dr. Dario Verdugo Binimelis, the physician resident of Easter Island. The student body also includes the son of Mr. Lorenzo Baeza, professor of the 72nd school located in the island. This group of students met daily, having Dr. Verdugo, his wife and Mr. Baeza serving as teachers.

I witnessed the development of the lessons of mathematics, Spanish, science and history. I was able to verify that the students are well prepared in all of their subjects.

---

[26] Secondary in Chile refers to higher level schools covering 1 through 12 grades, in contrast to Primary schools covering only through the 6th grade and normally used by children coming from poor families.

This teaching activity is well equipped with teaching materials, such as books, chalkboards, maps, charts, notebooks, diagrams, etc. All of this is worthy of applause and encouragement for the children as well as for the parents, who are their teachers. They have been able to overcome all the inconveniences that the conditions in the island have imposed from its distance and limited resources. This effort is a product of the strong yearning to educate their children. We salute this educational initiative leading to intellectual and social progress.

Héctor Poblete Cabezas
Inspector of Education
3rd District, Valparaiso – Chile

For us, this home schooling experience has left our family with fond memories and we are very proud that it turned out so well. It also increased our respect and admiration for teachers, who perform with personal sacrifices, and the amazing and noble mission of educating our children.

While we recall these memories of just a short period of this faraway time in our lives, I reflect, with Adriana, that we could not have had a more interesting and gratifying experience than teaching our children ourselves. This is how I described our educational initiative in my journal:

> "I expect that the principal fruits of this effort will
> materialize at the right time in the future. For the
> time being, they have been able to continue their
> school education without interruption, as if they had
> never left the traditional school in the mainland, and
> I venture to say that they may be performing better
> than their peers. I hope that the education and values
> that we have given them—*"que Dios quiera"*[27] that

---

[27] Que Dios quiera, meaning literally 'as God wishes', similar to 'God willing', is a common expression implying desire supported by God.

they always preserve—will lead to stronger family
union as well as appreciation for their parents. Later
on, when they establish their respective families,
they will realize that there is nothing better in this
world than a home with a strong union. A union that
constitutes this small and magnificent natural society,
"the family", nurtured with mutual affection and
respect, and one in which every member contributes
to foster an environment conducive to flourishing
spiritual development and economic well being."

As Adriana and I reread these old lines, I thank God that these
hopes have become a reality and we can verify, with joy, that the good
seed that we sowed developed in fertile soil. Each one of our sons is
living evidence of this. They have become distinguished professionals,
given us much joy, love and respect, as well as a large family which we
are enjoying with grandchildren and even great-grandchildren.

I should emphasize that in addition to the classes we taught
and with equally important purposes of personal development and
education, we held regular family meetings after dinner. In these family
meetings we would read about specific topics, have discussions and
exchange opinions about topics relevant to our family life, and encourage
opportunities while discouraging those things or behaviors that were
not desirable. Little by little these meetings became weekly and they
turned into the more formal "Verdugo-Gormaz Family Meetings", for
which we began to keep minutes in the "Family Book". In this book,
which we regard as a family treasure, one can read in the first few pages
the initial session outlining the basic guiding principles:

In Hanga Roa at 20 hours on Saturday the 10th day
of October of 1953 the members of the Verdugo-
Gormaz family assembled, under the presidency
of Dario Verdugo-Binimelis and acting secretary
Pedro Alberto Verdugo Gormaz, with the assistance
of Adriana Gormaz de Verdugo, Dario Verdugo

Gormaz, Roberto Verdugo Gormaz, and Gonzalo Verdugo Gormaz and they have come to an agreement to meet on Sundays in "Family Council", with the following purposes:

1st To promote the spiritual development of the family through God's love.

2nd To promote the love of the family through a closer union, trust and mutual help among all its members.

3rd To pay special attention to the intellectual, physical and economic well-being of the family.

4th To love one another in society.

5th To study, analyze and make a reality all the means needed to reach the above goals.

6th With these purposes it is therefore agreed:

To assemble weekly on Saturdays;

a) To alternate monthly the Presidency of the "Family Council" between the mother and father;

b) To have the children rotate the position of Secretary, monthly;

c) Decisions are made based on the majority vote. In case of a tie, the President will resolve the vote.

d) Special sessions can take place when required on the day and hour that is agreed upon.

The present rules can be expanded or modified by petition and a majority vote.

We found these family sessions to be of great value, and we continued them even after we returned to the mainland. This was the open forum, in which parents and children exchanged opinions, proposed solutions and formulated rules. When the family split up for natural reasons such as study abroad, work, or marriage, the regular reunions were discontinued, but even today with three of my sons living abroad, there have been many times when we found the opportunity for the six of us to gather. We have established special sessions utilizing the "Family Book", and as in the truly good old days, we openly shared our problems, our successes and aspirations. We continue to provide each other mutual support and every day we thank God for the continuation of this union despite the vast distance among the members of our loving family.

CHAPTER SIX

GEOGRAPHY AND CLIMATE IN RAPA NUI

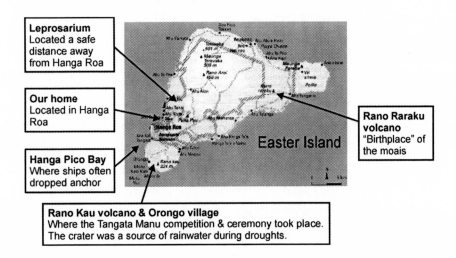

Leprosarium
Located a safe distance away from Hanga Roa

Our home
Located in Hanga Roa

Hanga Pico Bay
Where ships often dropped anchor

Rano Raraku volcano
"Birthplace" of the moais

Easter Island

Rano Kau volcano & Orongo village
Where the Tangata Manu competition & ceremony took place. The crater was a source of rainwater during droughts.

Those who visit Rapa Nui often speak of its "eternal spring," so many have accepted it as reality that its pleasant climate equates to that romantic season; however that is not the reality.

Easter Island is situated at latitude 27° south and longitude 110° west, so effectively it is just below the Tropic of Capricorn where the tropical region begins. The island is therefore in the subtropics, with all its climatic advantages and disadvantages. In relation to Chile, Easter Island is in the middle of the Pacific Ocean across from Chile's northern port of Caldera and at a distance of 2,600 miles from the port city of Valparaíso.

The island is shaped as a right-triangle, with the right angle pointing north-northwest. Its sides measure 16 & 18 kilometers, and the hypotenuse is 25 km., resulting in a surface of about 180 square km[28]. With this shape, I used the island as an example when explaining the famous Pythagorean theorem to my children: For a right triangle with short sides of length a and b and hypotenuse c, then $a^2 + b^2 = c^2$. My sons tell me that with the graphic description I used by cutting a paper map into the respective squares corresponding to each coastline of the island, they remember the essence of this theorem to this day.

Its peaks are formed by inactive volcanoes. Toward the southwest is the Rano Kao volcano with its impressive crater where the annual Tangata-Manu, "Bird Man" competition is held. Toward the east is the Poike, almost adjacent to the Rano Raraku volcano, which is of great archeological interest since it contains the quarry for the stones used for the construction of the moais. Toward the north, just below the Maonga Terevaca mountain[29] is the Rano Aroi volcano. The coastline of the island is mostly steep and rocky, with very few coves—which creates a challenge for ships to moor and to load and unload their cargo. The most suitable area for anchoring is Hanga Piko, making it effectively the "port" of the island right next to the village of Hanga Roa; although it's totally open with no protection against winds or rough seas. Whenever the sea gets rough, an anchoring ship has to lift anchors and begins circling the island from a prudent distance from the coastline. There are very few sandy beaches; the main one is Anakena across the island from Hanga Roa. It was a day excursion by Jeep to get there and our children loved this exploration.

---

[28] This is approximately 69 square miles, or three times the size of the island of Manhattan.

[29] The summit of the Maonga Terevaca is the highest point on the island, where one can see water 360° all around the island, providing a deep sense of solitude.

The soil of Easter Island reflects its volcanic origin, with very thin topsoil. Although there is paleontological evidence that in the distant past the island was covered by forests, today it has very limited trees, mainly *miro tahiti* and *makoi*. The loss of trees on the island has resulted from the erosion caused by using the island as a sheep farm, which, combined with the rain and strong winds, have removed substantial amounts of organic soil from its surface. You can also find fig trees, orange trees, acacias, and banana trees with their beautiful bright green leaves—those fruits were delicious and provided a healthy diet to the islanders and our family. I must point out that this is what one could appreciate during the 1950s, while we were residents of the island. The situation today has somewhat improved, as palm trees have been brought back to the island. There has been some reforestation of the famous *tolomiro* tree with its beautiful wood used for wooden carvings and the "talking tablets" called *rongo rongo*. Flowers were diverse and attractive. The most abundant and decorative species were called "tahitians", which were very fragrant, in addition to carnations, red bougainvilleas (which grew in two beautiful versions: reds and orange) and several other species.

With respect to the fauna there were plenty of horses, sheep, and some cows and pigs. Chickens were abundant. There were no pets or household animals such as dogs or cats on the island back then, but in our case the children treated their horses and some of the chickens as pets. They normally fed their horses banana peels by hand, which the horses liked very much. In the chicken coop, some hens felt so comfortable with Roberto that they would stand on his shoulder and he could even walk without them running away. My children had true rapport with some of the animals on the island.

There were plentiful crustaceans such as delicious lobsters of the type found in Australia and subtropical waters[30]. There was plenty

---

[30] There are two important families of edible lobsters. The Nephropidae, which include the American lobster (most abundant in Maine and Atlantic Cananda), have a pair of large claws and are found in the northern Atlantic Ocean. The Palinuridae or spiny lobsters (also called rock lobsters) lack the large claws and have spines over their bodies. They live in subtropical and tropical oceans.

of fish; the natives captured cod, tuna and other strange and colorful species of the area.

Easter Island does not have the clear differentiation of the four seasons as exists in continental Chile. The island has only two seasons: summer and winter, and both with an average humidity bordering 80%. Summer is warm with frequent pouring rainfalls and squalls, followed by a burning Sun. Winter is not as rainy and somewhat cool at times especially when the Aleutian winds blow with strength. The Aleutians are typical of the subtropical zones and were so useful during the days of tall sailing vessels.

The sea, as a good temperature buffer, caused the difference between day and night to be almost imperceptible. With respect to the temperature of the ocean, during the Pascuense summer (from October to May) it is always pleasantly warm. For those latitudes the cold Humboldt Current, which comes from the South Pole and affects Chile, does not touch the island. For the five months that last the winter, the ocean temperature cools off, but never as it is felt in Chile, and one can enjoy swimming year-round.

These Aleutian winds deserve a special mention. They are persistent westerly air streams common in the subtropical regions, and on Easter Island they swept vigorously. During the winter months we experienced them day after day, becoming annoying to the point of causing irritation. I believe that this was the only source of stress. To hear and feel the continuous whistling of the wind with such force, morning, noon and night, day after day, was something truly distressful. Our children would feel no desire to go outside, and the only entertainment inside for them was books—no radio, TV or telephone. And this wasn't the only byproduct of these winds; it affected life in other ways as well. The continuous winds had an adverse impact on the vegetation, as they normally carried moist air with marine salts, effectively burning the vegetation near the coastline—the *toroco* grass[31], the shrubs and sometimes even the trees. Following a few days of constant wind, it was disheartening to see such extensive brownish vegetation. The trees

---

[31] *Toroco* is the typical weed of Easter Island used to make Polynesian mats and roofs.

became bare with their branches appearing to reach out, pleading to overcome the forces of nature.

During the summer, while the temperature reaches a moderate 81° F, it feels substantially hotter on the island due to the high humidity. The clothing tends to stick to the body and even the sheets are uncomfortable at night. This sticky heat became unbearable during Sunday Mass, the only occasion for a gathering of people in an enclosed area. We could perceive the thick and dense air, and we would sense the most primitive blending of strange smells. The strong odor of human sweat reflected the heavy mutton diet of the islanders, and when mixed with the stench from the shortening used by the males as pomade for their hair, it permeated the church with a not-so-pleasant aroma.

The Verdugo family in front of their house, with the governor and Pascuenses

The high humidity is not only a problem of comfort because of having to deal with sticky clothing, but also because of its effects on a variety of other things. For example, if we were not careful with the sugar by storing it in hermetically sealed containers, it would be transformed into thick syrup with limited or no use because of its unpleasant flavor. Humidity showed up in other places as well. One day I noticed that a pair of shoes I had not worn for a while (since I normally wore espadrille sandals) were evenly covered by a thin layer of green mold, looking more like elegant existentialist suede shoes thanks to this humidity. The most troubling aspect of the humidity, however, was its impact on our dear books. We had to take care of them constantly and the children took turns weekly to move each of them from shelf to shelf and to brush them off to avoid any deterioration.

When the winds would eventually die down, how pleasant and marvelous was the dusk! Then we eagerly took advantage to go for family walks, or botanical excursions with the children, trying to classify the plants that we ran into, or to simply enjoy those magnificent sunsets. We then used our imagination to transform those sunsets with the various shapes of clouds into a glorious spectacle of "Pascuense Movie Theater".

The nights could also be extraordinary. The clear sky of Easter Island and the lack of urban lights allowed a magnificent vision of the stars almost unreal under the cupola of that gigantic planetarium. Within that grand spectacle I felt that I could place in perspective the petty selfish affairs and problems that we tend to blow out of proportion in our daily lives on Planet Earth. We could then appreciate a purity of life such as birth, love and death with the desires of God, without the interference from mundane minutiae. In those moments we could experience a glimpse of eternity.

But there were gloomy and dark nights as well. When I had to walk during the night to visit a patient for a house call, I experienced the sensation that I had to separate the shadows to advance, and then they would close back up behind me, oppressing my spirit. Additionally, there were occasional nighttime rainstorms with strong winds along with thunder and lightning plus the deep sound of the breaking waves. The feeling I experienced from this setting was similar to the fear from letting loose a pack of starving wolves. In nights such as these I prayed to God that I would not have to go out to see a patient for a home visit—but God did not always hear my prayers.

The rain on Easter Island deserves a separate commentary. In those days rain on the island had an enormous importance, since there was no infrastructure for drinking water. To begin with, rain was the *only* source of drinking water for the island. The volcanic origin of Rapa Nui with its porous soil and limited area prevents the accumulation of water, and the island is too small to support river formations. The island not only does not have rivers, but it doesn't even have small creeks—making it necessary to capture fresh water from the rain that falls on roofs and is stored in water tanks adjacent to each home. In addition to these man-made water tanks, there are two sources of water that are practical to use: some natural lagoons in the crater of the inactive volcanoes, of which the most important was in Rano Kao, and several caves on the island where water accumulated. When there was a lack of rain it was noticeable to see lower water levels in the caves. My wife endured great frustration with the droughts for her vegetable garden, which she kept with much devotion and care. When water did not fall from the sky, we had to say goodbye to fresh vegetables!

Fortunately, rain was generally frequent, but sometimes with very special characteristics: partial rains. We could see torrential squalls falling in very limited areas. When those squalls came close to home, how frustrating it was not to be able to capture their benefits. Other times we could enjoy the spectacle in the sea where the rain looked like a down-pouring curtain of water, while there would be sunshine in another spot. Under the intense semi-tropical rains, however, it did not look like rain was falling; rather it would appear that *the ocean had been elevated* and it was pouring all over the island. I have not seen such intensity of rain even in Southern Chile, which is known for heavy rains. Under pouring rain the dusty roads of Hanga Roa became rivers and the water ran with fervor, carrying along to the sea some of that valuable topsoil. Yes, the erosion that occurs on the island is not only the result of actions of mankind and the large sheep population, but it is also due to the strong winds and rain.

In periods of water scarcity it was disheartening to witness a dark cloud flying over our home with the promise of feeding our water tank and the garden—and then proceed toward the ocean where it would dump all its precious freshwater. On other occasions, it could rain on our next-door neighbors, while our vegetable garden would remain dry.

The Rano Kau volcano, filled with rainwater- most of which is covered with floating vegetation. Photo: Michael Wozniak

The worst drought we experienced was the infamous and painful five-month drought during August to December 1953. The first stage was a substantial decrease in the water levels in all domestic water tanks, to the point that we had to ration its use. We had to go to the ocean to bring water in buckets for cleaning dishes and also for use in the toilets. While in the beginning we used our limited rainwater to bathe ourselves, eventually we stopped using the bathroom sink entirely. Adriana discovered that the Lacón laundry detergent that we used did not break down in saltwater—and so, with her characteristic positive and resourceful approach to challenges, she simply had us bathe in the ocean with Lacón. While frankly the soap powder was not terribly appealing, it was another problem solved.

The dirty laundry began accumulating to such an extent that many families, including ours, had to form long caravans by horseback to go and launder the clothing in the lagoons of the Rano Kao crater. It was a full-day affair for our maids, who had to take food and other provisions.

For cooking we had to utilize well water from a few windmills. Those wells had been built around the island to provide water for sheep and horses. It had an unpleasant mineral and salty taste, not drinkable for humans, but it was adequate for cooking. Adriana did her best to camouflage the taste in her cooking, using as many herbs as she could from her precious dwindling collection she had brought from the mainland. The food prepared in this way didn't need to be salted, but for many people it caused diarrhea.

We remember with nostalgia the island's weather, with its advantages and disadvantages, its geography and its fragile geological structure. With the perspective of time, half a century later, I would give anything to return to live those marvelous days in which, close to our children, we would sometimes suffer a drought while at the same time take so much pleasure in the colorful sunsets and the awesome nights crowded with stars.

CHAPTER SEVEN

VESSEL IN SIGHT!

It is impossible not to recall with emotion the excitement that we experienced in those years with the rare visit of a ship to this small speck of land located in the middle of the Pacific Ocean.

To truly understand this excitement, we have to place ourselves in the environment in which the Pascuenses lived—when the only contact with the mainland was through shortwave radio and the annual vessel.

From continental Chile it took between seven to ten days for the crossing, depending on the vessel and ocean conditions[32]. The ship itself was not the sole motive for excitement, but rather what it brought. The ship meant arrival of basic goods, including flour to bake fresh bread, dried beans, and clothing, all of which was distributed by the island's Commissary. The vessel also brought presents to the few natives who had developed friendships with mainlanders on prior trips. We also received magazines and newspapers to bring us up to date on current events from that strange world that existed beyond the horizon. We received mail and presents from our loved ones, and parcels we had

---

[32] The very slow *Allipén* navigated at seven knots, and took 12 days to reach the island.

requested containing small items important to us: a good bottle of Chilean wine (absent from our table for many months), some chocolate, and other little things that, once on the island, acquired proportions of an oriental treasure.

There was also the arrival of other humans, with new faces and unfamiliar voices, telling us fantastic stories that perhaps the islanders could never envision with their minds. Lastly, among the passengers there were occasionally some Pascuenses returning from the mainland where they had gone as guests or stowaways, and they would relate in their own language their impressions and wonders of the continent. Because of all this commotion, the anticipation in the community started building up several weeks prior to the vessel's arrival; the kind of excitement one would experience if a spacecraft came to visit us from Mars.

Once the radio operator on the island got the news via telegraph, he would pompously announce the expected arrival date and then all preparations would fervently begin. The white people—*blancos* as the mainlanders were called—also shared this excitement.

The natives, with plenty of free time on their hands, picked tropical fruits, captured lobsters at night with torches, starched their clothing and began carving furiously to have enough "trading currency" for bartering with the visitors. Everyone got busy with their scissors and barber's razors to look good for the visitors with a short haircut. They whitened their cottages and *pircas* with powdered lime, performed home repairs and improvements, and a few with entrepreneurial interests prepared lodging for possible tourists (which were rare). The majority of visitors were public officials using the trip as a junket and came to the island with the "responsibility to resolve all its pressing problems"... The island's limited world of both natives and mainlanders was in unison for the big reception and upcoming events.

The arrival of a ship was a jubilant occasion and constituted the biggest party of the year; it far surpassed the celebrations of the Chilean Independence day or the anniversary of Chile's possession of the island, both events that the Chilean authorities tried unsuccessfully to emphasize. Those Chilean holidays were definitely not relevant to the natives. As the arrival date approached, most people anxiously searched the horizon just in case the vessel showed up early. Since the village of Hanga Roa is located at the west end of the island and the ship was sailing from the East, many islanders rode their horses to the other side to be the first to observe that small dot that gradually would become the long awaited visit. As soon as they spotted the coming ship, they would ride their stallions back to the village, galloping at full speed, to become the town criers announcing the good tidings.

When a few hours later the vessel would circle the island's triangle where the Rano Kao stands, and passing by the legendary islets Motu Iti, Motu Tautara and Moto Nui, it would proceed toward Hanga Piko where it would drop anchors. By then most of the population would have gathered at the modest pier and a small group of muscular males would jump into elongated and narrow boats to paddle fast and highly synchronized against the breaking waves in order to meet the vessel anchored a couple miles away.

Those aboard the ship could then observe in the distance the excitement of the population on the coast. Men, women and children, mostly dressed in white, would be running restlessly from side to side, like happy puppies. By then, the canoes that had gone to meet the ship had reached their destination after the treacherous crossing of breakers at the reefs, and their crews would climb the ship through hanging ropes and their brown faces would suddenly appear with smiles outside the guard rails greeting those aboard with warm handshakes.

The air would be filled with laughs, the sweet Pascuense language and the musical Polynesian salutation "*Ia Orana*". The gift of a pineapple or a small wooden moai would be the customary gesture to seal a friendship that began with "I am your buddy". This relationship would then constitute a limited partnership that on the one hand could involve giving away a horse (which nobody could take back to the mainland anyway) in exchange for clothing, soap and other miscellaneous goods from the mainland, all of which far exceeded the value of the original present offered by the natives.

During the ship's stay (normally from a week to 10 days) the island would be full of music, dancing, romantic adventures, wooden carvings of moais, lobsters and curanto meals, all in an almost carnival festive environment. For the visitor who intended to learn about life on the island during that stay, those days did by no means represent the daily life, and so they usually ended up acquiring an inaccurate view of the island and its people.

The visitors lived the emotions of a romantic episode during those short days on the island. Their imaginations stimulated during the long journey, and shaped by what is known about Polynesia through Pierre Loti, Gaugin, or the movies, would all contribute to a distorted image that subconsciously tended to remove them from reality.

The rhythmical and sweet Polynesian music would complete the glamour at the evening parties and the days would float by as in a charming dream. The visitors would watch the natives with leis around their necks dancing to the beat of the *sau-sau*[33], they would experience the deep blue transparent waters of the sea, they would taste exotic fruits. And some almond-shaped eyes of a pretty tanned Polynesian girl with sexy dancing hips would make them fantasize — and on occasion, live — an adventure of Polynesian love... The banana trees and the volcanoes with dormant craters, the soft and warm sand of Anakena beach where the legendary king Hotu Matua arrived, or the pink sands of Ovahe beach, plus the gigantic moais, reverential and sad, would complete the stage for those unforgettable days spent on a solitary island of the South Pacific.

The rest of the the year, Rapa Nui returned to its normal, more subdued mood with another face that is only known to those who have lived it—not so exuberant and smiley, but always with pastoral tranquility.

For our family, one particular visit was very special and emotional. It was the visit of the SS *Angamos*, a WW-II transport ship

---

[33] A Polynesian dance originating from Samoa

from the Chilean Navy which visited the island during August of 1953, an unusual occurrence as the regular annual ship came in December. In addition to her crew, a few tourists and the never-missing public officials, came my beloved father Pedro Verdugo-Cavada. My father was then 64 years old, and was a man full of life and with a big heart. He left my mother at home in Santiago and took a one-month sabbatical from his profession as an attorney to visit his distant "Pascuense family". He was gregarious with an expressive temperament, had a robust appetite for gourmet food, was a connoisseur of good cognac and a true aficionado of opera; he particularly admired Caruso. His sartorial expression reflected the conservative nature of the Chilean society: Getting casual on the island for him meant taking off his suit coat, but still keeping his starched white shirt and tie. My children affectionally adressed him as "Papa Peyo[34]".

The excitement that the ship's arrival normally brings to the population was multiplied several times for our family on this occasion. My father who was so dear to us, stayed at our home for several days. He would tell us about my mother, my brother who was a priest living in France for a few years, and my sister Carmencita, living with her family in Southern Chile. He gave us news about our relatives and friends, and shared his views about the economic situation in Chile.

We would channel all our family sentiments toward him: be with him, embrace him and kiss him. Even though so many years have gone by since that event, it is vivid in my mind and I can still experience the emotion that I felt then. Such emotion toward my father was expanded by his departure many years later on the other journey at the end of our terrestrial lives called by the Lord. I realize I cannot embrace him today to express my gratitude for giving me a life that, with God's goodwill, has been been so wonderful for me and my family.

During his stay with us we truly pampered him. We became his tourist guides as we tried to show him everything on the island. My wife Adriana ensured that he was well taken care of; knowing his

---

[34] *Peyo* is a diminutive for *Pedro*.

connoisseur habits for good food, she ensured that we had an ample supply of the very tasty Easter Island lobsters. Our children spent plenty of time with their Papa Peyo, enjoying his company, and I have kept several pictures memorializing the joyful occasion.

Visitors from the SS Angamos at the Verdugos' home - including Chilean writer Benjamin Subercaseaux, left.

In addition to my father, several interesting personalities came on the SS *Angamos*. These visitors included two well-known Chilean writers: Luis Merino Reyes and Benjamín Subercaseaux, and other people whom I knew well, such as my colleague and friend Jorge Guzman Polloni and Manuel Romani, Esq. Finally there were also two families that were being transferred to stay—they expanded our circle of friends from the mainland as we developed warm relationships with them: The representative from the Chilean Army, Captain Mario Salvago and his lovely family; and the newly appointed resident agronomist Efrain Volosky with his wife Eliana, a social worker from Santiago.

I must say that the visit of the SS *Angamos* was most remarkable and enjoyable, not only because of the quantity but also the quality of its passengers. Those days went by very quickly and it is extremely difficult for me to express all the sentiments that we experienced seeing my father on such a remote island. When emotions and feelings are too deep, we can only experience them, as it becomes virtually impossible to express them accurately in words.

The departure of the SS *Angamos* after its two-week visit to the island was very sad indeed. It was reminiscent of the same sadness that we sensed when we left the mainland. The departure of my father from the island touched everyone in the family deeply, as it distanced us again from our roots and loved ones back home.

Grandpa "Papa Peyo" while visiting the island, with
his four grandchildren and Adriana

Chapter Eight

Some Challenging Medical Encounters

Before we arrived on Easter Island my medical expectations were very high, since I was informed that I would be responsible for its small hospital, which although modest, had the required medical equipment and supplies to perform the necessary medical duties. Upon arrival, however, I discovered that reality was quite different. The "hospital" was a humble wooden structure with minimum facilities, equipment and supplies; water was collected from rain on the roof and stored in a cement tank—and there was no electricity.

This modest medical facility had two wards with six beds each, and with a sign at the entrance of each that pretentiously read "Ladies' Section" and "Gentlemen's Section". Additionally, there was a small multi-purpose clinic to perform certain "medical actions". (I think it would be an overstatement to categorize them as "medical *interventions*".) The surgical instrumentation was the bare minimum and the only procedure for sterilization was the use of boiling water. In this small clinic I performed several medical procedures such as: the stitching of open wounds, treatment of bone fractures by application of wet plaster (which could not be monitored through x-rays since such equipment was nonexistent), bandaging of sprains, removal of debris and foreign objects from eye injuries, miscellaneous cure procedures, and whatever other first-aid was needed for the islanders.

There was also another room in the hospital that had a primitive dental chair and a collection of forceps for molar extractions, and that was the only dental procedure that could be performed since there were no dentists on the island. Finally, there was a limited lab, which I was very proud of and where I spent long hours most days performing bacteriological and clinical work for the island population. Tests from all individuals of the island were done on a rotational basis, including healthy individuals as well as those with ambulatory leprosy (those with tuberculoid-type leprosy and negative nasal frotis for the Bacillus of Hansen). The objective of this initiative was to be able to determine leprosy cases as early as possible, and thus commence medical treatment up front, improving the probability of a cure. I relied on a magnificent German microscope in the lab which I had to use with light from a kerosene lamp. With the heat generated by this lamp I often felt I was roasting while doing my bacteriological analysis. In this setting I would spend long hours, surrounded by my medical gear and instrumentation along with the Bunsen flame, performing these bacteriological exams. I felt this preventive approach was essential to effectively research and manage the leprosy risk of the population.

This humble facility was situated right in front of the Hotu Matua Square, a short walking distance from our home. This square is the starting point of the principal street of Hanga Roa: a long strip stretching across the village and continuing on to Mataveri at the foot of the Rano Kao volcano, where the airport runway is located today.

I was truly a general practitioner but with one caveat: there were no referrals to specialists as occurs in our more advanced society.

As a physician I had the support of two male nurses from the Chilean Navy: a non-commissioned officer from the mainland and a Navy nurse from the island. Both nurses had excellent professional training, and they were gracious and courteous with our patients. Two additional native nurse assistants supplemented our medical team.

The first time I hospitalized a patient, I realized how impractical it was to segregate the rooms by gender. When patients were hospitalized they would bring along their entire family, along with mattresses so they could all sleep over to stay close to their sick family member. I was never able to convince the family members with medical rationale or appeals to authority that we could not allow that practice to continue. So in the end I had to accept this as a cultural reality of the island, and later in the rare case when a patient would be hospitalized alone without family companionship I would be most surprised. In fact, I found that patients would generally heal faster when accompanied by family members.

Hospitalizations did not represent the most serious medical problems. One of my biggest challenges was when I had to perform midwife duties to deliver babies—occasionally in the hospital but generally in their homes, where most women of the island gave birth. The difficulties were similar in both the hospital and at the homes, since both locations lacked sanitized conditions. While the expectant mother would lie on a mattress dimly illuminated by a nearby kerosene lamp, I only had modest instruments which were sterilized with boiling water. Fortunately I never faced puerperal infection or other types of clinical complications.

What I still remember with anguish was when, shortly after arriving on the island, I had to assist in the delivery of a baby from a mother who had been experiencing contractions for several hours without success. Upon examining her, I discovered with horror that this was a breech birth (where the baby was oriented in the wrong direction in the birth canal). This was something I had not seen since my internship as a medical student at the San Borja Hospital in Santiago. At the time I had enjoyed that internship so much that I thought about specializing in Obstetrics. Faced with this reality, however, I had no real experience in such a procedure. All I remembered was that in those cases there was need to utilize a procedure designed by a Madame Lachapelle over a hundred years earlier, of which I had a vague recollection. I immediately jumped onto my horse, Insipient, and galloped home to consult my small medical library which I used for questions and critical medical issues such as this. I quickly found the relevant material in the Obstetrics textbook and devoured it. This refreshed my memory on the theoretical aspects of the procedure for a breech birth, making me feel more comfortable, and I jumped on my horse to hurry back to the laboring mother. While riding back I prayed to God for his guidance. When I arrived at the patient's home I began my work immediately. By then I was calm, relying on my refreshed knowledge and on God, who gave me strength.

It seemed as if the labor lasted an eternity, and I sweat profusely from the anguish and the hot, humid climate. In the end, the baby was turned around into normal position and was delivered safely and was healthy. Following the delivery and the removal of the placenta, I lied down on the floor and because of the extreme stress I found myself crying. After this difficult delivery, I always said that if there was any doubt about having a guardian angel, that day I firmly believed in him, because without his supernatural help I could have not done what I did. In spite of the conditions in which this baby delivery took place, the outcome was perfect. My status and prestige among the islanders grew tremendously—everything that happened in the island, good or bad, was instantly communicated and perhaps with some added embellishment. The island had no secrets.

The other medical problem that I frequently faced was related to bone fractures. This pathology resulted mainly from falls from horses and from trees where the natives went to pick fresh figs or other fruit. To deal with a fracture without the support of x-rays was difficult and required keen skills. At the risk of coming across as ostentatious, of all the inferior fractures I treated no patient ended up limping once they were cured. This gave me enormous professional satisfaction and fulfillment.

One medical visit that I remember with compassion and some humor, was the time when a group of nuns, who helped manage the leprosarium, went for a swim in the ocean and one of them, quite young, fell along the rocky shoreline and dislocated her shoulder. I was called to treat her, and the suffering nun with her characteristic modesty was terribly shameful for being half-naked. With her dislocated shoulder, she had not been able to get fully dressed in her religious habit for my medical visit. With much modesty she tried covering herself, which she could not do. I had to examine her and then perform the necessary procedure to push the head of the humerus back into the cotyloid cavity in the clavicle at the shoulder. I cannot avoid contrasting the shyness of this young nun—a virtue that was also appreciated by most young girls in the past—with the absolute lack of modesty displayed by many young ladies today.

Eye care was another area I had to deal with. During the visit of the annual vessel after our first year, The Lions Club of Santiago donated corrective eyeglasses for those senior people suffering from presbyopia, the common symptom that causes people in their late 30's or early 40's to need reading glasses. I decided to keep the corrective lenses for those middle-aged and senior patients. But many younger Pascuenses thought it would be "cool" to wear glasses, so they would come to the hospital and request them, alleging that they could not see well. I had great difficulty convincing them that they would not see well with those prescriptions and therefore they could not take them. Finally, after much reluctance on their part they accepted, and I was able to keep the glasses for those older folks in real need. I concluded that vanity is certainly universal.

A case that I remember with great emotion was when a lady of advanced age came to be hospitalized alone and told me that she knew with certainty that she would be dying the following day at 4 P.M. I examined her carefully, and except for senility I didn't find anything that would make me think she would die soon. At her insistence, however, I let her stay in the hospital. The following day she asked her relatives to bring her the crown that she wore at her wedding when she was a young bride. Upon receiving her crown, she made herself comfortable in bed and, sure enough, at 4 P.M. she passed away placidly to meet her husband in heaven. How do we explain this?

I do not have an explanation, but I know that there are people in simple cultures who are able to anticipate their own death. When

I remember this event today, I experience an emotion in which peace, love and humility come together for everything that is unknown to us. At the same time this reaffirms my belief in the existence of God, who truly guides our destiny.

Dr. Verdugo at his hospital lab with his visiting father

Chapter Nine

Leprosy in the Island

While it is not my intention to do a comprehensive analysis of leprosy, an infectious chronic disease which is endemic to the island, in a book about our life on Easter Island it's necessary to provide some background on this infection, since it had a relationship to our lives.

To begin with, Chilean physicians have only a theoretical notion of leprosy, as fortunately it does not exist on the continent, so I had to brush up on my academic medical knowledge during our 12-day journey to the island on the the *Allipén*. Armed with my basic research, I could then approach this topic scientifically and rationally upon my arrival.

Leprosy is a chronic infectious disease caused by a bacillus, the *Mycobacterium leprae*; it is also known as Bacillus of Hansen in recognition of the Norwegian physician and bacteriologist who discovered it in 1869. It belongs to the same genus as the bacillus that causes tuberculosis, the *Mycobacterium tuberculosis* or Bacillus of Koch. Leprosy has a preference for the peripheral nerves and other regions of the body such as skin and mucosa.

It is characterized by lesions of the skin and peripheral nerves. Most complications are due to peripheral nerve involvement causing loss of sensation, which in combination with the skin being severely affected may result in extremities becoming deformed and eroded, leading to amputation in severe cases. The precise transmission of leprosy is uncertain. Close to 50% of the patients had a history of intimate contact with infected people; it is acquired principally within the family environment. The period of incubation for this disease is quite long, ranging from one to two years and even up to more than 40 years.

It is very difficult to study the penetration of this bacillus into the patient's body. Normal skin provides a natural defensive barrier against this infection. It's generally accepted that the germs can frequently enter through nasal mucosa. Some facts also support penetration through the lungs and vocal mucosa.

Once the organic resistance is defeated and the barriers of protection are overcome, the bacillus is carried via the lymphatic system to the ganglions, where they settle for a variable period and from where they disseminate afterwards.

Leprosy is classified into two types which are opposed—the so-called polar types—plus another undetermined group:

1. Lepromatous leprosy

2. Tuberculoid leprosy

3. Indeterminate leprosy

The Lepromatous type, at one end of the spectrum, is a generalized infection involving skin, mucous membranes and peripheral nerves with various degrees of numbness (sensitive neuritis.) The most common skin lesions are maculas, which are flat spots, nodules and plaques. When they infiltrate the facial skin, the patient appears with an aspect of a lion's face (*facies leonina*).

The Tuberculoid type of leprosy, at the other end, is revealed by one or a few pale, ("hypopigmented") macules with well defined borders and by patches that become insensitive to physical stimulus as they spread. On occasion the distal nerves become compromised. This tuberculoid leprosy occurs when the patient's immune system is able to fight the bacteria, making this type more benign.

The Indeterminate type of leprosy occupies the middle of this spectrum and manifests in compromises that reflect both polar forms.

Prevention is fundamentally achieved through the isolation of infected patients and the periodic check-up of the population to determine if they posses the Hansen bacillus in the nasal mucosa. Educational programs are also very important to disseminate the knowledge associated with hygiene, diet and infection prevention, thus enhancing the "cultural health" of the population.

I emphasize the importance of isolating infected patients and the early detection of the infection so immediate treatment can be initiated. In those years I utilized Conteben, a sulfa drug (a "sulfonamide"). It had a weak bacteriological impact and mostly acted by inhibiting the synthesis of substances that contributed to the microbial development. I prescribed doses of 100 milligrams daily, and never experienced complications or undesirable side effects. I must point out that there are no major revisions in the way leprosy is treated today. Medicine continues to utilize sulfonamides, but Rifampin is a commonly used medication today as well. This is primarily a bactericidal that unfortunately can produce serious toxic side effects. Among the sulfonamides there is now a drug called Clofazimine that can also produce certain adverse consequences, including skin coloration, making it cosmetically unacceptable especially for light-skinned patients.

Those patients with the more benign Tuberculoid-type leprosy and negative nasal results did not require isolation and came to the hospital daily. Alberto Hotus, the native Navy nurse, administered the medication to the patients. I remember him with much affection and admiration. He was very responsible, and in addition to being very dedicated he was an excellent professional. He also helped me as translator of Pascuense when necessary. Later in life, and after retiring from the Navy, Alberto has played an important role as defender of the interests of Rapa Nui and its people, even becoming mayor of the island.

For the patients interned in the leprosarium, in addition to administering the sulfonamides it was crucial to treat their injuries and take measures to prevent other infections. It was also necessary to provide sustenance to those who were physically and emotionally affected. Finally, there was need for great care for those who had become insensitive to physical stimulus and thus were exposed to further danger of injury, which could lead to blindness and amputations.

During my stay in the island, there were thirty-seven leprosy patients, about four percent of the population. Of those patients, thirteen were interned in the leprosarium and twenty-four were outpatients with a more mild non-contagious type. About one-third of the patients were women. It must be pointed out that leprosy in Easter Island was generally benign, in which the Indeterminate and Tuberculoid types predominated. There was only one patient with the more severe Lepromatous type.

This disease generated extremely conflicting feelings for me: pain on the one hand as well as joy on the other.

It was a profound experience for me when I met the leprosarium patients for the first time. I still remember when riding on my horse for a few miles toward the leper colony that first day. (Horseback riding was my normal means of transportation to reach the leprosarium.)

Because of my anxiety, I felt that this first horseback ride to the colony lasted forever—and when I arrived I wished that the place was even further away. I admit it: I was afraid. After getting into my medical gown and placing a protective mask over my mouth and nose, I went through the gates, upon which I saw myself surrounded by a group of men and women, some of whom were very young. They all greeted me with some fear. I was deeply moved not only by the effect of leprosy with their leonine faces, and others with amputated extremities and some crawling with great difficulty, but mainly by the fact they appeared to be lonely and abandoned by their loved ones. They were "prisoners" without defined timing or parole, and some were there for life. Their only crime was to have become infected with a disease for which the proud medical science did not have a definitive cure. What a great lesson in humility and empathy I received that day! At that moment I pledged not only to make the best effort I could with my limited medical knowledge and resources, but to give them all the compassion and love from my heart that I was capable of giving.

Ever since that first time, my visits to the leprosarium were made without fear, but instead with love and profound compassion. Quite often Adriana accompanied me, and the patients were happy with her visits as they generally felt isolated and rejected by the rest of the island community.

On one of those trips, Adriana, who was very athletic and somewhat equestrian, had a chance to show off her skills when the horse she was riding unexpectedly jumped and she fell off; but miraculously, she landed on her feet. Some Pascuenses who saw her amazing recovery speculated that she had been a circus performer on the mainland!

Although I say that I lost the fear of contamination of leprosy soon after my arrival, deep inside I did still experience fear, which I tried to conceal. A small mishap made this fear much more palpable for me. One day while galloping home from a medical visit, I (clumsy me!) fell off my horse. The fall resulted in a minor laceration on the top of my left hand, which I didn't pay much attention to. A few days later, however, I noticed a scar which stretched my skin and I began noticing some insensitivity in some of the fingers of my injured hand. I then began thinking about the connection between leprosy and the skin becoming numb. But while logic and scientific reasoning would say that such a conclusion was absurd, given the long incubation period of the Hansen bacillus, my subconscious was screaming: *Leprosy!* I even had a dream one night that I was being hospitalized in the leprosarium. I did not say a word to Adriana, since I did not want to alarm her, but I began as a precaution to maintain a distance from her and the children. Then one day the scar from my "hand with leprosy" broke away, upon which the sensitivity fully returned to my fingers. It's possible that the scar and related stretching of the skin affected some peripheral nerve endings, causing that symptom that concerned me so much. How happy I was to say goodbye to my nightmare of leprosy!

Although so many years have gone by since our life in Easter Island, I still remember with anguish those times in which I had to confine a patient in the leprosarium. The process was triggered when, during my frequent lab tests, I would detect a patient with nasal *frotis* (blood smear) positive. I would repeat the exam several times hoping to be wrong, and that forced me to stay for long hours with my tints of nasal *frotis* and my microscope illuminated by the kerosene lamp. Only when the bacteriological exam resulted categorically positive did I dare to tell the patient that they needed to be isolated in the leprosarium to avoid others becoming infected. This determination was more serious and painful than when a judge dictates a prison term. I don't want to even think about those nights that preceded the isolation of a patient. I thought about the suffering of the person, to be removed from his or her loved ones and the isolation that they would be facing. I asked God to help me in making the right decision and also for God to give strength to the unfortunate patient to accept his situation.

How different was my disposition when, instead of interning a patient in the leprosarium, I could release an inmate back to his family and community! This occurred when the treatment with sulfonamides was successful, as seen by clinical improvement and decisively negative results for the nasal *frotis* exams. I was overjoyed, thinking about the happiness the patient would feel to be able to reach freedom once again and rejoin his family. Everyone rejoiced; how wonderful it was for the relatives and the Pascuense community as a whole.

The good news was communicated to the patient and his family, who would organize welcome festivities after such a long separation. For the day of the release, friends and family would come in a caravan on horseback to meet the patient at the leprosarium's gate, located a few miles north from the village of Hanga Roa. Everyone wore their best Sunday outfits and the patient would walk out, say their farewells to those staying behind in the leprosarium and, with tears in his eyes, run to the ocean to take a dive of "purification". Upon coming in from the ocean, the released patient would receive his new clothing from his family, which would not always fit well. In those moments of reuniting, there would be warm hugs and emotional words of welcoming from those, who for such a long time—sometimes years—had only seen him or her from a distance.

Going back to town was boisterous and joyful and the patient's friends and family would prepare an *umu*[35] for the day. This *umu* would consist of a lamb specially sacrificed for this occasion, combined with fish, lobster and vegetables, all wrapped with banana leaves. In those days there was no alcohol in the island, so the happiness that was expressed in parties was genuine and natural. The melodic Polynesian music and the rhythmic dances were part of the celebration, and they normally lasted into the late hours of the night.

---

[35] This is the underground *curanto* meal – see Chapter 3

Chapter Ten

An Epidemic of Measles

The epidemic of highly contagious measles (Rubeola) that struck the majority of Pascuenses in late 1953 was an arresting and frightful experience for me and sparked enormous health fears throughout the island. On very few occasions can someone in the medical profession witness with such clarity the full lifecycle of an epidemic affecting the total population of a society: the initial onset, then taking hold and spreading, throughout such an isolated population that had been virgin and unexposed to many common infections and therefore lacking natural immunity against them. This was reminiscent of plagues that occurred in history back when immunization did not exist. This could unfortunately also become a reality with new infections for which we do not have medical solutions today.

As a result of the need to monitor the development of this disease as it spread throughout almost the entire population, I was able to use these data to analyze the demographic profile of the population and arrive at some interesting conclusions, which I discuss later.

Measles is an acute, highly infectious disease, caused by a virus. Close personal contact is the usual method of spreading the infection. In the early eruptive stage of the disease, it spreads out largely by airborne droplet nuclei from the nose, throat and mouth, so it is difficult to avoid contamination once the virus has begun to spread.

Following an incubation period of seven to fourteen days, the infection develops with a fever, coryza hacking cough, conjunctivitis ("pink eye") and very unique eruptions, called the Koplik's spots, on the inner lining of the cheeks which appear two to four days after the onset of symptoms. Within two days a characteristic rash appears, beginning in front and below the ears and on the neck, and spreading rapidly to the trunk and the extremities as it begins to fade away from the face. At the peak of the illness, the patients experience high fever (above 104° F) and they become quite ill. If there are no complications the fever falls in about three to five days. Measles confers lifelong immunity and children in early infancy are protected by placenta-based immunity.

There is no specific treatment for measles; bed rest is necessary as well as symptomatic therapy. Only in cases of complication with serious bacterial infections is an appropriate antimicrobial drug indicated.

The cause for this epidemic goes back to the arrival of a vessel in 1953, bringing along two natives returning to Easter Island. While they appeared to be totally healthy upon their arrival, they possessed the virus in an incubation stage. A few days later, the outbreak of measles appeared and spread throughout the islanders like igniting gunpowder. I instituted control procedures to manage this public health situation which ended up covering 771 cases, effectively the total native population at that time (793).

I later learned that these two Pascuenses had been in contact with children with measles just prior to boarding the vessel to Easter Island, and the incubation occurred during the eight-day journey to the island, developing the measles three to four days after their arrival.

The isolation of the island in which this infectious disease had never before been present, explained why the population had no immunity against this virus. In most societies, adults are immune because of prior immunization and infants acquire immunity from their mothers. The week these two Pascuenses brought the measles virus to the island, the infection began extending among the population in successive waves, eventually covering the population in its entirety. The *only* exceptions were the forty "mainlanders", nine natives who had resided in Chile, and the thirteen patients isolated in the leprosarium. As the last wave of patients came down with the measles, those who experienced it earlier had by then recovered, but we experienced a peak in which almost all the Pasquenses were bedridden, and many had serious complications.

This situation in which just about everyone was ill required that the few of us who weren't affected had to coordinate our efforts to take care of and feed the population. We, the "mainlanders", prepared food that was later distributed to most homes. For my part and with the assistance of my staff, I had to take care of patients day and night. The treatment was principally symptomatic, and we only prescribed antibiotics to those experiencing complications. To those with pneumonia we administered penicillin, and for those with otitis (ear inflammation) and similar complications we utilized sulfa drugs. It was necessary to be very careful with the limited therapeutic supplies that we had available. We had to go from house to house, not only to provide medical attention, but also to encourage the Pascuenses and to reassure them; since in addition to feeling so bad they could not comprehend what had happened to them that caused such massive disease. The majority of the islanders were treated at home since it was not possible to bring over 700 patients to the hospital. I only hospitalized infants of less than one year old, fearing pulmonary complications. We put them in a heated room with steam to facilitate breathing. This youngest group was made up of 30 baby boys and 19 baby girls, of which one-third experienced pulmonary complications resulting in two deaths.

Within the next-youngest group, covering ages one to 14 years old, there were 336 patients (190 boys and 146 girls) of which eight (2%) experienced pulmonary complications, resulting in the death of a two-year old toddler.

The next age group included those from 15 through 74 years old, comprising 378 patients (189 women and 189 men). Of those, 33 patients (9%) suffered pulmonary complications, and one 61-year old passed away. Everyone in the senior group (including those above age 65) contracted the disease (three men and five women). Among these seniors a 75-year old died.

In summary, this was a devastating epidemic for the natives, something they had never seen before in their generation. It affected 97% of the population. In all, 57 patients, or 7%, suffered pulmonary complications and five islanders passed away. Fortunately, due to our proactive efforts, the mortality rate was less than 1% of the population.

Once the epidemic receded, the serenity of the Pascuense life returned to the island, with all the lasting speculation and commentaries of what had occurred, of the suffering, of the deaths and of the helping hand that the mainlanders provided for everyone during these trying times.

The shock that this measles epidemic caused among the population was not only due to its severity, but also to the fact that the Pascuenses were used to experiencing benign cases of flu a few days after vessels visited the island and lasting for a few days. This condition was labeled by the natives as "*ko-kongo*", which is simply a common cold that is produced by various types of viruses brought by the mainlanders for whom they had no immunity. This "severe case of *ko-kongo*" (measles) that year was very different from the usual *ko-kongo* that they had always experienced with the visits of vessels.

As a byproduct of this broad epidemic challenge that I faced, I was able to analyze the demographic distribution of the population. The right-hand man who I had for this task was my friend and assistant Alberto Hotus. I was therefore able to study the various age groups of the island by gender, which are summarized in the table below:

Native Population in 1953 by Age Category

Age	Males	Females	Total	Percent
Up to 14 years	220	165	385	49%
15 - 64 years	205	195	400	50%
65 and above	3	5	8	1%
Total	**428**	**365**	**793**	**100%**

Total population, including 40 mainlanders: **833**

In 1953 the population was very young—nearly one-half of the islanders were less than 14 years old.

As shown in the next table, by 1992, the last census before this book was first published in Spanish, the population of Easter Island had more than tripled. We can also see a trend toward an older overall population. Both these trends reflect the large influx of mainlanders.

Total Island Population in 1992

Age	Total	Percentage
14 and younger	950	34%
From 15 to 64 years	1,763	62%
65 and older	106	4%
Total	**2,819**	**100%**

Since1992 we can see the rapid growth trend continuing. Looking at 2002, the latest year of a census, the island population grew further to close to 3,800, up over four times the level of 1953. This significant population growth has resulted from the large influx of mainlanders, reducing the Pascuences to a minority 40%:

Long-term Trends of Population and Cultural Mix

	1953	**1992**	**2002**
Total population	833	2,809	3,791
Pascuense Pct.	95%	42%	40%

The island is clearly losing its native Polynesian identity. In the year 1953, 95% of the population was Pascuense. The 2002 census identified that the Pascuense mix dropped substantially to 40% of the population, less than half the proportion of 1953.

Should this trend of a reduced Pascuense presence continue we can anticipate that in another 50 years the native population would effectively be absorbed by the mainlanders, with all the implications that it represents regarding the threat to the culture's preservation and heritage.

CHAPTER ELEVEN

THE PSYCHOLOGY OF
THE PASCUENSES

To understand the psychology of the natives during the 1950's, we must remember the extreme isolation of those living on Easter Island. As I described earlier, the only regular contact with the mainland was through the annual sailing of a vessel chartered by the Easter Island Company, and communication through the naval radio station, which was primarily used for official matters and sending meteorological reports to the mainland. There were some occasional visits to the island by ships from the Chilean Navy, and once we received unannounced a highly luxurious British cruise liner, the *Caronia*[36], for a few hours. On that cruise the tourists would not even disembark for sightseeing at the celebrated Rano Raraku volcano with its recognized moais. Obviously such a sophisticated ship could not risk disembarking upscale passengers on an unknown island—a remote speck of land with no landing infrastructure, accommodations or transportation, with no

---

[36] During 1954, the *Caronia II* from the British Cunard Lines embarked on what was probably her most enjoyable and unusual itineraries with a Japan and South Pacific cruise of 99 days from New York, with two transits of the Panama Canal, and calls to Easter Island on her way to Samoa, Fiji, and New Zealand.

knowledge of the language, and personal safety issues such as health and native behavior.

Many islanders of course had conversations with the short-term visitors, which did not really expand their knowledge frontier beyond the island very much. Consequently, we can say that they lived in virtual isolation from the exterior world; and the few external things that the islanders knew about were embellished as "fantastic" and "amazing" in endless, not always coherent, conversations among themselves.

The social economic environment on this island without currency or material possessions led to an egalitarian society in which the distinction between rich and poor was nonexistent. They did not view themselves as poor, as they had no exposure to the consumerism and higher living standards of the mainland that they would otherwise compare themselves to—what economists call the "Demonstration Effect"[37]. Similarly, the notion of social classes did not exist either; they acted with dignity and they considered each other as equals. People from the mainland were also viewed as equals and they treated us very casually and informally[38]. When meeting them, regardless of status or age the Pascuenses would begin with a friendly "Eh, I am your buddy". They would then expect to create a permanent linkage of friendship with that new acquaintance.

There was no alcohol, tobacco, and of course no drugs.

I would venture to say that the Pascuenses were basically good-natured and innocent people; they had not been touched much by modern society. There was no selfishness and there was no desire to possess material goods. I have come to think that material progress

---

[37] Demonstration Effect represents the effects on the behavior of individuals caused by observation (through TV, movies or traveling) of the actions of others and their consequences. The term is particularly used in economics to describe the fact that developments in one place will often act as a catalyst in another place. Such effect tends to increase material needs and desires when witnessing societies with higher living standards.

[38] While the regular language is a Polynesian dialect derived from Tahiti, they spoke Pidgin Spanish, and they only used the familiar "tu" rather than the formal "usted" as would be used extensively in Chile.

may limit the possibilities of achieving truly sound and fraternal human relations.

I believe the Pascuenses of that period were genuinely happy. They enjoyed a mental state of serenity coming from a harmony that they had with their surrounding environment. They were never busy nor did they experience personal loneliness, and they appeared to be satisfied with what little they had, which was viewed as communal property for sharing based on need. The islanders were content in the way they carried out their lives. Such simple and somewhat primitive happiness overflowed to the mainlanders living on the island, including our family. We would adapt ourselves to the environment, fully accepting its limitations and seeking the beauty and enjoyment of life by focusing on nature. To be able to appreciate nature at its best: a night full of stars, a sunset, the birth of a flower, the smile of a child. It appears almost impossible to fully appreciate these simplicities of life in our urban cities where we become totally immersed in "things".

The Pascuenses had a limited conception of how to deal differently depending on circumstance or rank; everybody was the same—including animals in some cases. It was a very child-like and naïve behavior. I recall when I was quite busy one afternoon in the hospital taking care of a patient when a Pascuense walked in interrupting me to complain, "*Taote*, I was in the hospital's front yard picking a fig off the tree to eat it, when your son Roberto's white horse came and ate the fig out of my hand." (Roberto fed his horse often by hand.) I told him not to be disrespectful and he should not interrupt me while I was busy. I advised him that he should deal directly with the horse in resolving this problem, and not with me. I remember looking out the window to see the Pascuense approach the horse, which was very tame and slow moving, and he proceeded to punch the horse on its chest. The horse neighed, turned around slowly and kicked him gently but squarely on his rear end. The Pascuense, somewhat frustrated, yelled a few words and left without eating more figs. He perhaps felt the issue was closed, but not to his satisfaction.

The Pascuenses simply enjoyed life as it existed for them, and this simple style began influencing our family life. The islanders acted naturally without conventionalisms or pretensions. They were complacent with no important projects to undertake, and "timelines" were unknown. Natural food from the earth was plentiful, the sea was an ample source of healthy seafood and families were entitled to free weekly rations of lamb. Everyone had a little cottage, and clothing came from the mainland in the form of donations, including Navy uniforms that were no longer in use. Shoes were rarely worn and they did not care—as a matter of fact they felt uncomfortably restrained in shoes.[39] While fashion did not appear to be relevant for the Pascuenses during regular days, Sunday Mass and the arrival of a ship provided a stage for them to display their unique garments. It was humorous to see on those occasions some islanders wearing casual pants and old white spats over bare feet left behind from a German vessel that stopped off at the island briefly during World War II.

All of this constituted a sound and firm foundation upon which the psychology of the natives rested.

The Pascuenses were friendly, spontaneous and faced everything with a calm that at times would even bother us. There was an expression that was used frequently: "*akare-no*", which represented a blend of "just leave it there" and "don't bother" (or the typical British, "not to worry"). In most cases when we asked them for something, their common answer was "*akare-no*", which meant "not important and not now, but perhaps in the future if I feel like it". I recognize that when the task was accomplished, the islanders generally did it well, and there were no consequences to not having accomplished it on a timely basis.

---

[39] As an anecdotal fact, my children outgrew the shoes that we brought along from the mainland. I improvised as a shoemaker and with great effort I made them sandals utilizing old tractor tires. Despite my initiative, they felt it "not cool" to wear such ugly heavy sandals and they ended up adapting very well to walking barefoot. The challenge was upon our return to the mainland—by then they had grown accustomed to not wearing shoes; and shoes now felt very tight and uncomfortable. To this day, all of them wear wide-shoe sizes, as their feet had adapted to the rough rocky soil of the island.

The notion of "time management"—doing things quickly and within a defined time frame, a notion so well accepted in our western culture—was totally incomprehensible to the Pascuenses. As a physician I have always experienced being short of time in mainland Chile; the multiple and competing demands for our time has become a reality of the "civilized world". The fact that I normally walk briskly was curious to the islanders and they always asked me, "Why do you walk so fast, Taote?" The truth was that it was difficult for me to respond rationally to this question, because it was not necessary to be in a hurry on the island, unless there was an emergency case to attend to, which was rare. Soon I began walking at a slower pace, and it allowed me to more fully enjoy the beauty that nature had to offer everywhere, which I did not quite appreciate before.

The lack of opportunity for the islanders to acquire goods such as clothing or something else they happened to need appeared to be a rare problem. When they wanted to acquire something, they would just pick up goods that were in the "possession" of others. This was not viewed as petty theft, but simply as a natural act to utilize something that was not being used by the person "owning" it. While there was individual privacy, the underlying philosophy was that goods were available to the community, and those who had the greatest needs at the time could have them. So things were "owned," but only for as long as the "owner" needed them. In this environment, goods could rotate from person to person, as we do often within our families.

This arrangement worked well for the Pascuenses at that time, because their small community really was more like a big, extended family in practice. A person may have "his" tool or personal item taken from him by a neighbor, who might later pass it on to someone else, but he knew he'd be able to get it back whenever he needed it.

I recall receiving two cases of wine from one of the shipments from the mainland. While the cases were in transit to our home from the Anga Piko pier, many Pascuenses helped themselves to most of the bottles, leaving us an "adequate stock" of five bottles for the rest of the year. They could not conceive of one family such as ours consuming all of those 24 bottles at once. The thought that we would save most of the wine for later did not even occur to them. Later that day, we could see many people walking around the village of Hanga Roa drunk, as they were not used to alcohol, and they never concealed this action as it was considered totally appropriate.

Within their family relationships the Pascuenses were affectionate with their spouses and loving with their children. The children were happy, free, and they were never treated with violence. Whenever they were mischievous, they had a common expression of acceptance: "that's the way the poki's (children's) life is". They used this philosophy for raising children, reflecting high tolerance, understanding and love.

The vocabulary used by the islanders was plain with simple nouns, limited adjectives and verbs without conjugation—their communication was straightforward, explicit and without inhibitions. I remember that shortly after arriving to the island, while walking under a full moon one night we saw a group of natives gathered at the Hotu Matua Square, singing with their guitars and dancing to Polynesian songs. We decided to get closer and hung around to watch. We noticed a girl, somewhat chubby, who was standing by herself without dancing. When my wife asked her why she would not join in the dance, she simply replied with a smile and no inhibition, "I don't dance because my butt is too heavy". That's the way it was: things were expressed precisely and directly without ambiguity.

It was common to witness groups of islanders gather around in a crouched position squatting on their heels to chat for long hours with highly expressive movement of arms and hands, laughing with a contagious enthusiasm, although I had no idea what they were talking about. They were enthusiastically socializing among themselves without having to be concerned about image or pretensions. The isolation, combined with the expressions of admiration for the moais and other rich archeological treasures by most visitors to the island, gave the islanders a very high self-esteem, as if it transferred the cultural heritage to their personalities. Some Pascuenses felt very proud and had the perception they were individually known throughout the world. I remember when the Mayor of the island, Pedro Atán, who was one of the best artists for carving wooden statues, would simply state with no modesty: "I am indisputably the best at carving wooden statues on this island," adding, "and I am fully aware that my carvings are known throughout the world". These perceptions and mindset reflecting a high self-esteem were quite prevalent, to different degrees, by many Pascuenses.

There is an aspect of the Pascuense mentality that is difficult to understand in depth, and is related to the fact that over many generations they have been immersed in a highly superstitious world. The Catholic religion, while highly embraced by the population, has been unable to displace superstition. When we lived in the island, the chaplain was the German priest and historian, Father Sebastian Englert, who with much wisdom knew how to deal with this environment without alienating the islanders' views and beliefs. Fr. Englert simply moved with patience and made them accept Christian beliefs gradually. The natives had inherited a belief in bad spirits, who reside in different parts of the island, to which they did not dare visit at night. These bad spirits, known as *Tatanes,* resided principally in the Puna Pau, a small volcanic hill near the village of Hanga Roa. Facing the *Tatanes,* however, were the *Aku-aku*s, a type of guardian angel, acting as neutralizers against the evil spirit of *Tatanes.* This superstition made the Pascuenses reserved and secretive at times, and thus they did not feel comfortable revealing certain aspects of the island with high archeological interest, as they feared the potential consequences from *Tatane*s for openly disclosing those sites.

In summary, the Pascuenses were good-natured people, genuine, without envy, rarely confrontational, and with whom one would like to maintain everlasting friendly relationships. It was an isolated society but without isolated individuals.

Epilogue

As we often experience ambivalence in our lives, the farewell from the island was both a sad and joyful occasion. We were saying goodbye to so many friends, to my dear patients from the leprosarium, to our humble little island house that we came to love so much, to our *Liceo* into which we poured so much love and dedication to educate our children. We were also saying farewell to the island with its dormant volcanoes, to its ocean with clear and temperate waters. We were principally saying goodbye, however, to an important chapter of our family life. It was a remarkably rich experience, in which we came to know and understand each other much better, and it strengthened further the foundation of our unity—going well beyond our blood relationships. We became more united by the love developed through collaborative work and by the close family kinship that we all experienced in the island.

Our family, at the same time, was happy with the anticipation of the joy of being reunited with our parents, brothers and sisters upon our return to the mainland. We would also be reunited with our mainlander friends and we would be back in the comfort zone of our familiar habitat. Particularly, I was excited to return to my hospital, with more resources, a greater variety of medical cases to treat, clinical discussions and knowledge-sharing with my colleagues. All this would contribute to an environment conducive to improving my clinical knowledge and enhancing further my medical professional development.

Lastly, although we had to return to struggle with the inconveniences of urban life in Santiago and the need to use money again to purchase so many necessary and unnecessary things, we were returning to our familiar surroundings where our roots were, which we missed at times while on Easter Island.

Now, as more than half a century has gone by, I remember with nostalgia our Pascuense life. Perhaps we have idealized it a bit, since human beings fortunately tend to forget more easily the unpleasant experiences and retain the pleasant ones. However, life is made up of darkness and light, sadness and happiness, of moments of excitement and others of indifference. If one learns how to accept and balance all these elements, we then advance much in achieving true happiness.

We observe the past, but we also appreciate our present. The goals that we have set for our children have been fully met, and now in our age of retirement we enjoy peace and the happiness of watching our children, grandchildren and great-grandchildren, all of whom are an extension of our lives.

In regard to "our island", we see that the fears the moai expressed in its monologue (chapter 4) have become reality. As shown in the following table, while during the 1950s the island had a population of about 800, the National Institute of Statistics reports in its last census of 2002 that the level almost quintupled to about 3,800:

Island Population and Pascuense Mix

	1953	1992	2002
Native Population	793	1,185	1,516
Mainlander Population	40	1,634	2,275
Total Population	833	2,819	3,791
Percent of Pascuense Population	95%	42%	40%

There is a substantial decline of the Pascuense population mix, from 95% fifty years ago to less that half the population today. This enormous population increase accompanied with a dramatic alteration in the cultural balance reflects the heavy migration from the mainland. I am concerned that this demographic shift is having adverse consequences for preserving the cultural heritage of this tiny Rapa Nui.

At a symposium titled "Chilean Doctors in Easter Island," held in 1988[40], Dr. Juan Grau expressed concern that the Pascuense population could gradually decrease further, adding: "It is in our hands to stop or accelerate the disintegration of the Rapa Nui culture." He was making a strong plea to the Chilean authorities for managing rationally the immigration of mainlanders to such a small and faraway community that is so incredibly rich in heritage.

I would have liked in this book, if I had the mandate to do so, to have the Governmental authorities implement the necessary public policy measures to protect the Pascuense culture. This would involve not only managing the influx of new mainlanders to the island, but also creating appropriate incentives for their return to the mainland. I refer mainly to a policy of gradual substitution of natives holding public jobs instead of mainlanders. In other words, the policy would be to encourage a reversal of the current trend and thus return to a social structure characterized by having a majority native population. The current structure, if not handled properly, will eventually drown out what little there is left of the Pascuense culture, and the Rapa Nui language could eventually disappear. The western culture, represented mainly by the "Chilean mainlanders," exported many of its bad habits and has created the necessity to earn money and to elevate socially; now the island society experiences socio-economic divisions between rich and poor. The Spanish language is fundamental to obtaining a job, which motivates its learning, as well as English because of all the tourists. Meanwhile, the Rapa Nui language is being abandoned since it is not viewed as useful for employment and making money. Adding to that is the lack of an educational policy and protection of the Pascuense cultural heritage. The overwhelming influence of the mainland will end up totally absorbing the Pascuense values and culture, including its sweet language, spoken well by adults but which only a small portion of children are fluent in today.

---

[40] A Symposium held in commemoration of the 100th anniversary of the annexation of the island by Chile

Through the press and television, we are now aware that alcoholism and crime have finally arrived on the island. Its society has developed a demographic makeup with economic classes, segregating between rich and poor. While horses were used in the past for transportation, as distances are short, it is now rather crowded with recreational vehicles and noisy motorcycles contaminating the tranquility that the islanders used to enjoy. In other words, "civilization has arrived" with its motor vehicles, its television programs with violence, with its urge for consumerism and all its implications. As happens on the mainland, the struggle to earn a living is evolving towards having to impress the neighbor. With all this "progress" and increase of the mainlander population, I ask myself: "Are the Pascuenses happier today than they were in the past?" While it's not possible to quantify, I am afraid the answer is likely to be "No."

I learned of a medical initiative undertaken by the Chilean Air Force in 1997 in which they found among other pathologies: hypertensions, heart diseases, and other chronic conditions. Thus, the pathology of the islanders is becoming a mirror to the medical landscape that we have in continental Chile and most "civilized societies." In other words, the civilization, with its defects and by changing the lifestyle, has transplanted to the island the pathology of the western culture. During our stay in the 1950s I never saw any arterial hypertension among the population and I never had to treat a cardiovascular condition.

It is my wish that the Government of Chile become mindful of what is occurring in the island. I insist and reiterate not only that they must not send more mainlanders to work there, but that they should actually take measures aimed at reducing the number of public officials stationed there. I also urge that they protect the archeological heritage, the Pascuense culture and the Rapa Nui heritage. If corrective policies and actions are not taken, it could all disappear, and that would be an imponderable loss to society.

While finishing this book I think with nostalgia about the mysterious Rapa Nui, the lonely and distant land that their first inhabitants baptized with the melodic name *Te Pito O Te Henua*, "the belly button of the world". I pose several questions to myself again: Archeologically speaking, what is this island? Was it perhaps the peak of a mountain belonging to an ancient continent that drowned in the rising waters of the South Pacific with the receding of the last ice age? Or is the island perhaps a byproduct of violent volcanic eruptions that took place in the bottom of the ocean millions of years ago? Where did the original inhabitants with their culture really come from? Did they come from the West or from the East? Or from both directions, as appears to be the case. What was the meaning of its moais and monuments? What inspired them to design these statues and build them in large numbers, and when did all this occur precisely? What do the writings of the mysterious tablets of *Kohau Rongo Rongo* say? Would the authenticity of the Pascuense culture eventually disappear as a result of the isolation that they experienced in that past and now is being threatened by the overpowering forces of western values and lifestyle? Can we accomplish both the advantage of modern life, while fully preserving the heritage and culture of the island?

The archeology, ethnology and geology of Rapa Nui continue to a large extent to be a mystery without answers, making its study more fascinating.

As a conclusion, I now reflect that my family and I could never have attended a better university to learn about life than by having resided in such a minute land lost in the middle of the Pacific Ocean... a tomb from a mysterious civilization, rocking in a cradle by the murmur of the ocean. This is our beloved and unforgettable Rapa Nui—which truly shaped our lives forever.

Afterword:

The Sons Reflect on Their Island Experience

The author's four sons wanted very much to share independently their personal impressions regarding the impact that the Easter Island experience has had in their lives.

In the following pages their thoughts are provided in order of age (they are about one year apart from each other):

Pedro Verdugo

Background:

- *He currently lives in Sao Paulo, Brazil where he is the founding shareholder and CEO of Software Ltda, a successful software company in the country. He has three children.*
- *He graduated with an Engineering degree from the University of Chile and later obtained a Masters' in Science at the University Of California at Berkeley.*

I believe that my life in Easter Island while I was growing up and as I entered my teenage years (between 12 and 14 years of age) helped shaped my character in several ways:

- By being the oldest of four brothers, I was normally assigned many important tasks for my age, such as: responsibility to maintain and repair the electric generator at home, act as a butcher and carve meat from the dead lamb that was dropped at our doorstep each week from the island's commissary, provide technical support for our ham radio equipment, often drive the stick-shift Jeep assigned to my father for chores, etc. All these duties were necessary in such an isolated place which encouraged my sense of **responsibility**.

- The lack of resources in a place connected with the mainland only once a year obligated all of us, as a family, to develop **creativity** to improvise and/or put together basic goods—such as shoes from used tires, soaps, dye using flowers from the island, oil lamps, etc.

- Without doubt, the island life was a school of **tolerance**, by being exposed to social customs so different from ours, leading to a peaceful and harmonious living environment.

It was a period in which we learned substantially more than if we had attended a conventional school by having our parents as teachers 24 hours a day.

To me this was a very happy period in my life.

Dario Verdugo Jr.

Background:

- *He presently lives in West Bloomfield, MI, USA. He recently retired as a senior Executive at DaimlerChrysler Corporation and founded a financial advisory firm: Value Creation Initiatives, LLC. He has three daughters.*
- *He graduated in Economics from the University of Chile and later obtained his MBA at U.C. Berkeley. He also attended Cambridge University in England as a visiting Fellow.*

I feel the influence from my two years in Easter Island was profound across several areas of my life:

- Appreciation of the true value of a family union – touching me as child in my formative family and later impacting my new family that I have helped raise as a father. The four of us brothers communicate among ourselves and with our parents regularly, despite being spread across different countries. I have also developed a deep sense of appreciation for the care, education and guidance we received from our parents which has been valuable for raising my own family, parenting with love and logic.

- Unconventional and creative thinking – Having been transplanted to such a different environment, I learned that there are many ways to approach life. This has also helped me foster creative thinking for problem solving.

- Faith on managing uncertainty – When my parents decided to jump on the Easter Island opportunity, it was a pure leap of faith. I have learned to listen better to my gut feelings, within a rational framework, in making choices when faced with uncertainty.

- Having been in an elitist and somewhat privileged position within the Pascuense society we learned to hold to high standards that would justify such perceived status.

- Cultural understandings and adaptation – I have been able to improve my understanding of diverse cultures, and adapt better to different environments—a big plus when I "repotted" from Chile to the U.S. during my twenties.

Roberto Verdugo

Background:

- *He is the only son who stayed in Santiago. He is the principal shareholder and founder of Inegración de Actividades "Integra", a relevant exporter of seafood products from Chile. He is a former undersecretary of fisheries in the Chilean government. He has five children.*
- *He graduated in Fisheries and Marine Sciences from the Catholic University of Valparaíso.*

The couple of years I spent in Easter Island during some of my formative years represented a significant milestone in my life. That experience contributed to the development of valuable dimensions important for success, both personally and professionally:

- Expanded my capacity **to adapt to diverse and unexpected conditions.**

- Enhanced my **ability to improvise** when faced with unexpected and changing conditions.

- Helped me appreciate much more the **value of a united family.**

- Gave me a better appreciation for **understanding the idiosyncrasies of other cultures.**

- Provided me with a better understanding in the value of **acting creatively** and not necessarily in accordance with pre-established and conventional thinking.

Gonzalo Verdugo

Background

- *He resides in Cambridge, MA, USA. He is a Partner at Computer Sciences Corporation Consulting Group where he specialized in business and technology strategy. He has four children.*
- *He graduated in Economics from the University of Chile where he also received his Master of Science in Business. He completed the International Teachers Program at INSEAD, France, and attended the Doctoral Program at Harvard Business School.*

My two years in Easter Island were perhaps the most formative of my life. As a child I was forever imprinted by this early experience, making the island the special place I have never forgotten.

Life on the island came with the complete lack of amenities we take for granted in our "civilized" world. There was no opportunity for social contact outside our immediate family, not with friends, schoolmates or even extended family. This led us (or forced us) to turn to our core family for all our social and emotional needs. Without stores, we had to turn to what the island provided for sustenance—our garden and the sea for food, and our rainbarrel for water. The lack of amusements such as radio, TV (which didn't even exist in Chile then), movies or magazines, made me rely on our twice daily swims in the ocean, playing (and fighting) with my brothers, roaming and discovering the island, and our family evenings together for entertainment.

At my young age, this basic life was happier and more enriching than what living in the city could possibly have provided, giving me a clear sense of the things in life that really count. Over the years, this experience has allowed me to appreciate my life as it unfolds through the eyes of a child.

For this, I thank my parents for following their hearts and their muse.

Glossary of Pascuense Terms

ahus. Base of moais used as tombs.

Anakena beach. Beach where King Hotu Matua and his settlers landed on the island.

curanto. Chilean covered-pit oven, similar to the Polynesian *umu* (see below).

Hanau Eepe. "Long-ears". The second wave of settlers to the island.

Hanau Momoko. "Short-ears". The original settlers to the island.

hanga. A bay.

Hanga Oteo. Oteo Bay.

Hanga Roa. The main village in Easter Island. *Roa* means long, so Hanga Roa is a long bay.

hare paenga. Typical Polynesian dwelling.

Hiva. Name of the country where, according to tradition, the Polynesian immigration of Hotu Matua came from. Nowadays this name means any continent or foreign country. See also *Tangata Hiva*.

Hotu Matua. Also known as "King Hotu Matua," the leader of the first settlers of Easter Island.

Hotuitis. Early tribes dedicated to farming.

kumara. Sweet potato. A very common food staple for the natives.

Make Make. God the creator.

mako'i. An island tree (Thespesia populnea), the fruit of this tree, or any tough inedible fruit.

mako'i nau opata. Sandalwood fruit.

manu taras. Native birds whose eggs were used for the Tangata manu competition.

Maonga Terevaka. Highest mountain on the island.

miro. Wood, stick; also (probably improperly) used for "tree".

miro huru iti. A shrub.

miro tahiti. A tree from Tahiti (Melia azedarach).

moai. The large stone statues for which Easter Island is world famous. These monoliths were carved during a relatively short and intense burst of creative and productive megalithic activity from compressed volcanic ash. The largest moai erected, "Paro," is almost 10 meters (33 ft) tall and weighed 75 tons. One unfinished sculpture has been found that would have been 21 meters (69 ft) tall and would have weighed about 270 tons. About 95% of the 887 moai known to date were carved out at the quarry of the Rano Raraku volcano, where 394 moai still remain visible today.

ngaru. Body surfing using a small flat board.

pircas. Stone walls erected from loose volcanic rock, seen along most roads on the island.

Poki bahine. Girl

Poki hiva. Child from the mainland. The Verdugo boys were *poki hiva*.

Poki tane. Boy

Rano Kao. Largest inactive volcano, with a large crater.

Rano Raraku. Famous volcano where most moais were carved out and erected.

Rapa Iti. Small island or islet.

Rapa Nui. The native name for Easter Island.

rongo rongos. Wooden tablets with early writings.

tangata hiva. Adult male foreigner, adult male from the mainland.

tangata kava kava, also *moai kava-kava*. Small wooden statue of a thin man with projecting ribs.

Tangata manu. Bird man. From *tangata*: man; and *manu*: bird figure (like the drawings or wooden figures once found in caves and houses). Also the annual competition to select the island's chief where a representative of each clan would dive into the sea and swim to the islet of Motu Nui to retrieve an egg laid by a *manu tara* bird.

Taote. Medical doctor having a priest-like stature.

tatanes. Bad spirits.

Te Pito O Te Henua. Name given to Easter Island by its original natives, meaning "the belly button of the world" or "the center of the world."

tolomiros. Early trees on the island. Later they were used extensively by the natives for carving figures, mainly miniature moais. Also, the wooden carved figures themselves.

toroco. Typical island weed (long and strong).

totora. Straw mats made out of *toroco*.

Tu'uaros. Early tribes dedicated to fishing.

tupas. Primitive huts.

umu. A Polynesian oven dug in the ground in which food is cooked over heated stones; or a meal or banquet cooked in such an oven. Similar to the Chilean *curanto*.

vaka. Canoe or small boat.

Vaka A Hiva. Hotu Matua's wife.

vaka hiva. A boat from a distant land.

About the Author

Darío Verdugo-Binimelis was born in Concepción, Chile in 1913. He studied medicine at the University of Concepción and University of Chile. His early professional years were spent as medical officer in the Chilean Navy, an organization that he has held in the highest regard and remembers affectionately. Subsequently he worked in the hospitals in Viña del Mar and San Borja in Santiago.

In late 1952, he was selected to be the resident Physician in Easter Island. He later obtained a degree in Public Health from the University of Göteborg under the auspices of the Swedish Government. Subsequently he joined the World Health Organization, spending several years in Central America, Indonesia, India, and Egypt.

He has been president of the Rotary Clubs of Viña del Mar and Providencia in Chile and he has held leadership positions in the Municipality of Providencia, one of the Metropolitan Areas of Santiago. He also was the chief medical officer at the Superintendence of the Social Security Office in Chile.

He is active in several medical and charity organizations (Capacitas Chile and Salvecor, where he was one of the co-founders). He is an enthusiastic supporter of medical doctors' rights and their professional interests within Chile, in his capacity as General Advisor to the Chilean Medical Association (Colegio Médico de Chile). Until recently he was a member for many years of the office of ethics for the Chilean Medical Association.

Currently he serves on the Board of Directors of the Medical Association of Retired Physicians of Chile.

.

Printed in the United States
85439LV00004B/92/A